The Lover of a Subversive
Is Also a Subversive

POETS ON POETRY

Annie Finch and Marilyn Hacker, General Editors
Donald Hall, Founding Editor

New titles

Meena Alexander, *Poetics of Dislocation*
Kazim Ali, *Orange Alert*
Martín Espada, *The Lover of a Subversive Is Also a Subversive*
Sandra M. Gilbert, *On Burning Ground: Thirty Years of Thinking About Poetry*
Grace Schulman, *First Loves and Other Adventures*
Reginald Shepherd, *Orpheus in the Bronx*
Reginald Shepherd, *A Martian Muse: Further Essays on Identity, Politics, and the Freedom of Poetry*

Recently published

Elizabeth Alexander, *Power and Possibility*
Alfred Corn, *Atlas*
Ed Dorn, *Ed Dorn Live*
Annie Finch, *The Body of Poetry*

Also available, collections by

A. R. Ammons, John Ashbery, Robert Bly, Philip Booth, Marianne Boruch, Hayden Carruth, Amy Clampitt, Douglas Crase, Robert Creeley, Donald Davie, Thomas M. Disch, Tess Gallagher, Dana Gioia, Linda Gregerson, Allen Grossman, Thom Gunn, Rachel Hadas, John Haines, Donald Hall, Joy Harjo, Robert Hayden, Edward Hirsch, Daniel Hoffman, Jonathan Holden, John Hollander, Paul Hoover, Andrew Hudgins, Laura (Riding) Jackson, Josephine Jacobsen, Mark Jarman, Galway Kinnell, Kenneth Koch, John Koethe, Yusef Komunyakaa, Maxine Kumin, Martin Lammon (editor), Philip Larkin, David Lehman, Philip Levine, Larry Levis, John Logan, William Logan, William Matthews, William Meredith, Jane Miller, David Mura, Carol Muske, Alice Notley, Geoffrey O'Brien, Gregory Orr, Alicia Suskin Ostriker, Ron Padgett, Marge Piercy, Anne Sexton, Karl Shapiro, Charles Simic, William Stafford, Anne Stevenson, May Swenson, James Tate, Richard Tillinghast, C. K. Williams, Alan Williamson, Charles Wright, James Wright, John Yau, and Stephen Yenser

For Amy —
Another subversive —

Martín Espada

The Lover of a Subversive Is Also a Subversive

October 29 2010

Subversive Is Also a Subversive

ESSAYS AND COMMENTARIES

THE UNIVERSITY OF MICHIGAN PRESS

Ann Arbor

A CIP catalog record for this book is available from the British Library.

Library of Congress Cataloging-in-Publication Data

Espada, Martín, 1957-
    The lover of a subversive is also a subversive : essays and
commentaries / Martín Espada.
        p.   cm. — (Poets on poetry)
    ISBN 978-0-472-07147-0 (cloth : alk. paper) — ISBN 978-0-472-
05147-2 (pbk. : alk. paper)
    1. Espada, Martín, 1957—Authorship.   2. Poetry—Authorship.
I. Title.
PS3555.S53Z46   2010
811'.54—dc22   2010030292

Acknowledgments

Some of this material originally appeared in the following publications, to whose editors grateful acknowledgment is made: *Hanging Loose:* "Blessed Be the Truth-Tellers" (poem); *Latino and Latina Writers, Volume 2* (Scribner's, 2004): "Blessed be the Truth-Tellers: In Praise of Jack Agüeros" (revised); *Naked Punch* (UK): "The Lover of a Subversive Is Also a Subversive: Colonialism and the Poetry of Rebellion in Puerto Rico"; *The Massachusetts Review:* "The Lover of a Subversive Is Also a Subversive: Colonialism and the Poetry of Rebellion in Puerto Rico"; *Poets Against War Newsletter* (online): "Seers Unseen: Poets of the Viet Nam War"; *Quay* (online): "A Branch on the Tree of Whitman" (revised); *Southword* (online): "I've Known Rivers: Speaking of the Unspoken Places in Poetry"; *Walt Whitman Quarterly Review:* "A Branch on the Tree of Whitman" (revised).

Dedicated to the memory of
Alexander "Sandy" Taylor (1931–2007)
and
Adrian Mitchell (1932–2008)

Contents

The Lover of a Subversive
Is Also a Subversive

Through Me Many Long
Dumb Voices
The Poet-Lawyer

I am a poet-lawyer.

The phrase *poet-lawyer* conjures up the image of a half-human, half-beast from ancient mythology, a peculiar creature with the head of a poet and the body of a lawyer. Poet-lawyer Archibald MacLeish reflected on this dilemma:

> Although a Law Review editor might reasonably be expected to end up as president of a bank or head of the Natural Gas Association, he has no right to turn himself into a poet. Why? I don't know, though I have often asked. People shuffle their feet and light a cigarette and look away and you walk back to Harvard Yard wondering if you really are queer after all.

According to another poet-lawyer, Tim Nolan, poets are considered "bohemian, irresponsible, free, flighty, subject to brilliant inspiration, aloof, poor, garroted, soulful, irrelevant," whereas lawyers are considered "masterful, composed, certain, needling, dogged, practical, insistent, combative, annoying, overdressed." (I am all these things.)

These two quotes appear in the foreword to a book called *Off The Record: An Anthology of Poetry by Lawyers,* which weighs in at 732 pages. (I argued with the editor that any anthology of poetry by lawyers should be called *On the Record,* to no avail.) Clearly, there is common ground between bards and barristers which goes beyond a fascination with language or the use of words as weapons. In my experience, that common ground is advocacy.

The tradition of advocacy in North American poetry goes back to Walt Whitman. In #24 of "Song of Myself," Whitman declares himself an advocate, but also insists on the primacy of other voices, long silenced:

> Through me many long dumb voices,
> Voices of the interminable generations of slaves,
> Voices of prostitutes and of deformed persons,
> Voices of the diseased and despairing, and of thieves and
> dwarfs,
> Voices of cycles of preparation and accretion,
> And of the threads that connect the stars—and of wombs,
> and of the fatherstuff,
> And of the rights of them the others are down upon,
> Of the trivial and flat and foolish and despised,
> Of fog in the air and beetles rolling balls of dung.
>
> Through me forbidden voices,
> Voices of sexes and lusts . . . voices veiled and I remove
> the veil,
> Voices indecent by me clarified and transfigured.

One of Whitman's greatest disciples was a poet-lawyer: Edgar Lee Masters. Masters was not only a lawyer, but an accomplished lawyer. From 1903 to 1908, Masters was the law partner of Clarence Darrow. (Darrow was a devotee of poetry himself; he published essays on Whitman and Omar Khayyám, among others.) Like Darrow, Masters often represented the poor, the powerless, and the unpopular.

As a poet, Masters labored in the shadow of his law practice, in part because he would sometimes publish under a pseudonym: Webster Ford. All that changed with the publication of *Spoon River Anthology* in 1915. For years it was the most widely read book of poetry in the United States.

Spoon River Anthology is a series of 244 poetic monologues, in nineteen linked narratives spoken by the dead of Spoon River cemetery. Masters took names and other information from the Spoon River and Sangamon River cemeteries in Illinois where he grew up, combining fact, fiction, imagination, and speculation. *Spoon River* reveals the underside of small-town Midwestern life, a rebuttal to the idealized fable of small-town America still packaged and sold today in one political campaign after another. Here there is greed, lust, betrayal, corruption, poverty, addiction, war, rape, and murder. The rich dominate the poor; men impose their will on women; white people brutalize the few who aren't white.

Through it all, Masters is the advocate. He subscribes to Whitman's decree that the duty of the poet is to "cheer up slaves and horrify despots," identifying with the most marginalized and despised citizens of *Spoon River*, condemning the powerbrokers.

These persona poems were clearly written by a practicing lawyer. The language is often similar to that of an affidavit: written in the first person, direct and clear, telling a story, attempting to persuade. In the practice of law, an affidavit is a sworn statement in the voice of the witness, but the statement is frequently written by the lawyer. The poet-lawyer of *Spoon River* must speak in 244 voices.

Many of these are Whitman's "long dumb voices"; those who were silent in life speak in death. There is the voice of "Yee Bow":

> They got me into the Sunday-school
> In Spoon River
> And tried to get me to drop Confucius for Jesus.
> I could have been no worse off
> If I had tried to get them to drop Jesus for Confucius.
> For, without any warning, as if it were a prank,
> And sneaking up behind me, Harry Wiley,
> The minister's son, caved my ribs into my lungs,
> With a blow of his fist.
> Now I shall never sleep with my ancestors in Pekin,
> And no children shall worship at my grave.

There is advocacy here, but no consolation: Yee Bow is as lonely in the graveyard as he was in the schoolyard, as lonely in death as in life.

Some of these poems have a startling immediacy and relevancy. "Harry Wilmans" is a soldier fighting for U.S. occupation forces in the Philippines at the turn of the twentieth century, convinced, perhaps, that the Yee Bows of the world were about to overrun the United States:

I was just turned twenty-one,
And Henry Phipps, the Sunday-school superintendent,
Made a speech in Bindle's Opera House.
"The honor of the flag must be upheld," he said,
"Whether it be assailed by a barbarous tribe of Tagalogs
Or the greatest power in Europe."
And we cheered and cheered the speech and the flag he
    waved
As he spoke.
And I went to the war in spite of my father,
And followed the flag till I saw it raised
By our camp in a rice field near Manila,
And all of us cheered and cheered it.
But there were flies and poisonous things;
And there was the deadly water,
And the cruel heat,
And the sickening, putrid food;
And the smell of the trench just back of the tents
Where the soldiers went to empty themselves;
And there were the whores who followed us, full of syphilis;
And beastly acts between ourselves or alone,
With bullying, hatred, degradation among us,
And days of loathing and nights of fear
To the hour of the charge through the steaming swamp,
Following the flag,
Till I fell with a scream, shot through the guts.
Now there's a flag over me in Spoon River!
A flag! A flag!

Harry becomes universal; he could easily be a soldier killed
in Iraq. Our leaders still make a fetish of the flag, for the same
purposes. Harry's voice echoes the many letters written home
by U.S. troops during the war in the Philippines, a war that,
according to historian Howard Zinn and others, left at least two
hundred thousand Filipinos dead. Masters, who opposed the
First World War as well, earned the wrath of right-wing patriots
with poems like "Harry Wilmans."

Masters left the law for literature in 1920, and reserved his
greatest contempt for a legal system at the service of the rich
and powerful. Here is "John M. Church":

I was attorney for the "Q"
And the Indemnity Company which insured
The owners of the mine.
I pulled the wires with judge and jury,
And the upper courts, to beat the claims
Of the crippled, the widow and orphan,
And made a fortune thereat.
The bar association sang my praises
In a high-flown resolution.
And the floral tributes were many—
But the rats devoured my heart
And a snake made a nest in my skull!

John M. Church, for Masters, represents the worst elements of
the system he left behind. Note the name *Church,* alluding to an
entrenched social institution with its own laws, and the parody of
legal language in the use of the word *thereat.* Of course, Masters
has total control of this imaginative universe, which explains the
presence of the rats in the heart and snake in the skull, cosmic
retribution for a lawyer who was a rat and a snake in life.

The judges in Masters's universe fare no better. "Judge Selah
Lively" is a prime example:

Suppose you stood just five feet two,
And had worked your way as a grocery clerk,
Studying law by candle light
Until you became an attorney at law?
And then suppose by your diligence,
And regular church attendance,
You became attorney for Thomas Rhodes,
Collecting notes and mortgages,
And representing all the widows
In the Probate Court? And through it all
They jeered at your size, and laughed at your clothes
And your polished boots? And then suppose
You became the County Judge?
And Jefferson Howard and Kinsey Keene,
And Harmon Whitney, and all the giants
Who had sneered at you, were forced to stand
Before the bar and say "Your Honor"—
Well, don't you think it was natural
That I made it hard for them?

Judge Lively, who rises to his position of authority by serving the most powerful citizen of the town (Thomas Rhodes), abuses that authority by making decisions based on a laundry list of grudges rather than any sense of right and wrong under the law. The petty, bitter voice in the poem no doubt echoes voices Masters heard in the courtroom over the years.

In the world of *Spoon River,* there exists the possibility of redemption through compassion. This is true even for the most arrogant of lawyers, who believe in the rule of law at the expense of justice. Witness the epiphany of "State's Attorney Fallas," who says:

> I, the scourge-wielder, balance-wrecker,
> Smiter with whips and swords;
> I, hater of the breakers of the law;
> I, legalist, inexorable and bitter,
> Driving the jury to hang the madman, Barry Holden,
> Was made as one dead by light too bright for eyes,
> And woke to face a Truth with bloody brow:
> Steel forceps fumbled by a doctor's hand
> Against my boy's head as he entered life
> Made him an idiot.
> I turned to books of science
> To care for him.
> That's how the world of those whose minds are sick
> Became my work in life, and all my world.
> Poor ruined boy! You were, at last, the potter
> And I and all my deeds of charity
> The vessels of your hand.

Edgar Lee Masters died in 1950, his reputation and finances in steep decline. Nevertheless, based on *Spoon River Anthology,* Masters—and not Wallace Stevens—can legitimately be called the foremost poet-lawyer of the twentieth century. (Stevens was a lawyer in the employ of an insurance company. He was not an advocate, either as a poet or a lawyer, and kept the two lives separate.)

My own poetry of advocacy bears the influence of Whitman and Masters, but also springs from my legal experience. I graduated from Northeastern University Law School in 1982, and even-

tually became a tenant lawyer, serving as supervisor of Su Clínica
Legal, a legal services program for low-income, Spanish-speaking
tenants in Chelsea, Massachusetts, outside Boston. Chelsea was
the poorest city in the state, with the poorest housing stock. We
handled eviction defense, conditions cases, injunctions to fix the
heat or exterminate rats, and trained students from Suffolk University Law School to do the same.

I published three books of poems during my six years at Su
Clínica. As with Masters, voices spoke first to me, then through
the medium of the poems. While waiting for my cases to be
called, I would sit on a staircase in the courthouse, scratching
poems on a yellow legal pad. One day I encountered the following "found poem" on the bathroom wall:

> *Courthouse Graffiti for Two Voices*
>
> Jimmy C.,
> Greatest Car Thief Alive
> Chelsea '88
>
> *Then what
> are you doing
> here?*

There were voices in the courtroom too:

> Mrs. López showed the interpreter
> a poker hand of snapshots,
> the rat curled in a glue trap
> next to the refrigerator,
> the water frozen in the toilet,
> a door without a doorknob.
> *(No rent for this. I know the law
> and I want to speak,*
> she whispered to the interpreter.)
>
> *Tell her she has to pay
> and she has ten days to get out,*
> the judge commanded, rose
> so the rest of the courtroom rose,
> and left the bench. Suddenly
> the courtroom clattered

with the end of business:
the clerk of the court
gathered her files
and the bailiff went to lunch.

Sometimes the Spanish voices spoke back with a few strong words in English, the language of the law:

She leaves the office
rehearsing with the lawyer
new words in English
for the landlord:
Get out. Get out. Get out.

Like Yee Bow, many of these voices belonged to silenced immigrants who one day could bear their silence no longer, and cried out:

The lawyer nodded through papers,
glancing up only when the girl awoke
to spout white vomit on the floor
and her father's shirt.
Mi vida: My life, he said,
then said again, as he bundled her
to the toilet.

I left the practice of the law in 1993, due to deep budget cuts in my program. I chose to leave rather than force out another attorney, a friend of mine who emigrated to this country from Chile after he talked his way out of being shot by a firing squad. He was born to be a lawyer.

I made a transition into the English Department at the University of Massachusetts at Amherst. However, I never stopped being a lawyer. Still influenced by that way of seeing the world, I teach poetry workshops in various places using *Spoon River Anthology.* This usually involves bringing my workshop group to a cemetery and turning them loose amid the headstones.

Once, instead of bringing the workshop to the cemetery, I brought the cemetery to the workshop. This was the brainstorm of Rich Villar and Fish Vargas.

Rich Villar and Fish Vargas are the co-directors of an organization called Acentos in the Bronx. Acentos stages readings and workshops in places where poetry supposedly does not belong. In May, 2009, we brought the *Spoon River Anthology* workshop to the Savoy Room at Hostos Community College in the Bronx. Vargas issued a memorable announcement ("If I hear your cell phone go off during this workshop, I will personally drag you out of this room by your hair"), and then the workshop began. Villar describes it in his *Letras Latinas* blog:

On the walls hung 112 photos of headstones from St. Raymond's Cemetery in the Bronx. Martín's workshop revolved around Edgar Lee Masters's *Spoon River Anthology*, a book of persona poems in the voices of the dead. Masters took the names from the headstones of Spoon River Cemetery. The Acentos workshop was about to do the same for St. Raymond's.

Espada started with a half-hour lecture on the life of Edgar Lee Masters, along with a reading of poems from the book itself. Some of the poems were in conversation with other poems. Most of them were highly speculative about the dead person's occupation, demeanor, relations, and relationships to the other dead people. So, taking these cues, and keeping in mind things like birth dates and death dates, names, proximity to other headstones, and a large dose of speculation, 78 workshoppers were sent wandering around the room in search of personae to write about, and through.

On this night, with Professor Espada, Latinos and Latinas were present in large numbers in the workshop . . . and on the headstones. This led to a great deal of poetry in Spanish, English, and code- switch: Investigations into the nature and results of machismo. Investigations into the youth of St. Raymond's Cemetery. Conversations among the dead and the living. Monologues. Speculation. And some unvarnished truth: twelve headstones were people Fish knew personally.

We ended the night with an open mic so large that we had to draw out participants from a hat (mine) . . . Surrounded by the denizens of St. Raymond's, with a fresh *Bronx River Anthology* in minds and in hands, a night of fellowship and goodwill among poets of all skill levels, all ages, all ethnicities, finished up a full hour behind schedule, and no one cared. Except, of course, for the intrepid cleaning crew at Hostos. (Yes, we helped them out.)

For Masters, this was a homecoming. In early 1944, he ended up in a Bronx nursing home after he was found suffering from malnutrition and pneumonia at the Chelsea Hotel. When the workshop poets of Hostos stood to read their poems, one by one, the voice of Masters could be heard through them. Now, however, the voice was Puerto Rican or Dominican. The voice spoke Spanish, or some combination of Spanish and English. The voice came from an immigrant grandparent, a forgotten actor, a drunk driver, or the driver's victim. The voice was the same. The voice had changed.

Edgar Lee Masters lives. In the Bronx. In Spanish.

The Lover of a Subversive
Is Also a Subversive

Colonialism and the Poetry of Rebellion in
Puerto Rico

My great-grandfather, Buenaventura Roig, was the mayor of Utuado, a town in the mountains of Puerto Rico. When he died in 1941, thousands of mourners flocked to his funeral. Almost fifty years later, my father and I searched for the grave of Buenaventura Roig.

We never found it. Instead, we wandered into a remote cemetery, high up in the mountains, with row after row of stones dated between 1950 and 1953. These were men killed in a faraway place called Korea, among the 756 Puerto Ricans who died fighting for the United States in the Korean War.

My father, Francisco Luis (Frank) Espada, was also a Korean War–era veteran. He fought another war, on a different front, refused service at a segregated diner in San Antonio, Texas, jailed in Biloxi, Mississippi for refusing to sit at the back of the bus, subjected to apartheid in the same country he was sworn to defend.

What the dead in that Utuado cemetery and my father had in common is that they were born in a colony of the United States, where the inhabitants cannot vote for President and have no voting representation in Congress, yet can be drafted to fight and die in the wars of the United States. Puerto Rico is the oldest colony in the world: four centuries under Spain and more than a century under the United States. In five hundred and seventeen years, Puerto Rico has not determined its own destiny for five minutes.

In the early years of U.S. occupation, poet and political leader José de Diego wrote, "Puerto Ricans do not know how to say no." Yet, he pointed out, "the 'no' of the oppressed has been the word, the genesis of the liberation of peoples." De Diego warned: "We must learn how to say no." He set the tone for a century of Puerto Rican poets to come.

The poets of Puerto Rico have often articulated the vision of independence, creating an alternative to the official history of the kind propagated by occupiers everywhere. They have been imprisoned for their words and ideas, despite the rhetoric of free expression favored by the United States. They have taught the next generation the arts of resistance, so that even poets living in the United States and writing in English continue to clamor for the island's independence.

Puerto Rico is a political anachronism, a throwback to the days of gunboat diplomacy and the handlebar mustache. On July 25th, 1898, U.S. troops landed at Guánica and seized the island as a prize of the Spanish-American War. General Nelson Miles, a decade removed from the Indian Wars and the capture of Geronimo, promised Puerto Rico "the blessings of the liberal institutions of our government." That government handed the economy over to four North American sugar companies, collaborating in the exploitation of the labor force; imposed a series of North American governors appointed by the President; established a military occupation; forced English on the public schools and the court system; and repressed the *independentistas,* or pro-independence citizens of the island.

In the 1930s, the world sugar market collapsed, and the economy of Puerto Rico collapsed with it. There was, as historian Kal Wagenheim put it, "virtual starvation." Julia de Burgos, who would become Puerto Rico's most beloved poet, gave voice to the rage and bewilderment of the population when she wrote (in the translation by Jack Agüeros):

> Where is the little one who in rickets unleafed his life?
> Where is the wife who died of anemia?
> Where is the vegetable patch she helped plant, she dead
>   today?
> Where is the cow?
> Where is the mare?
> Where is the land?

The reference to "the little one" is not a coincidence. Julia de Burgos was the eldest of thirteen children in rural Carolina, Puerto Rico; she watched six of them die. The poet proposed a revolutionary solution:

> sharpen your hoe
> whet your machete
> and temper your soul.

> Descend from the cliffs
> and cross the fields drunk with cane.
> Come close!
> . . . .
> Look at the sugar mills:
> There is your dead wife!
> Contemplate the savage banquet of the machines
> grip your hoe
> and proceed
> and say: "'Til I return!"
> Come close!

The movement for independence reached its peak in the mid-1930s with the rise of the Nationalist Party, spearheaded by a fiercely brilliant Harvard lawyer, Pedro Albizu Campos. Albizu led a cane-cutters' strike in 1934, "a machete march / of calloused hands and feet," in the words of Julia de Burgos, herself a committed Nationalist. Two years later, Albizu and seven other leaders were rounded up by the U.S. government and charged with seditious conspiracy. In fact, the U.S. law of seditious conspiracy has been applied almost exclusively to Puerto Ricans.

There were two trials in 1936. The first resulted in a hung jury. The second resulted in conviction, but only after the prosecutor hand-picked a jury of ten North Americans and two Puerto Ricans. (The prosecutor, Cecil Snyder, flashed his list of jurors at a cocktail party to none other than Rockwell Kent, the renowned artist, who made this information public.) The defendants were sentenced to terms ranging from six to ten years for, in essence, conspiring to overthrow the government of the United States on a Spanish-speaking Caribbean island. Albizu, the most dangerous man in Puerto Rico, would spend most of the next three decades incarcerated.

13

The protests continued into the following year. In Ponce, on Palm Sunday, 1937, police fired on a Nationalist march, killing twenty-one people and wounding more than a hundred and fifty. One *independentista* recalled: "My mother left in a white dress and came home in a red dress."

This was not the language of the official story. The bloodletting was characterized on the front page of the *New York Times* as a "Nationalist Riot." However, an American Civil Liberties Union lawyer, Arthur Garfield Hays, conducted his own investigation: the police, in fact, were the ones who rioted. Hays published his report in *The Nation* magazine, exposing the incident that came be known as "La Masacre de Ponce," or the Ponce Massacre.

The collective memory of such events, repressed in the interest of colonial power, must be perpetuated by word of mouth, by song, and by poetry. When Bolivar Márquez, a Nationalist shot down and dying in Ponce, wrote in his own blood on the sidewalk, *Long Live the Republic! Down with the Assassins!*, Julia de Burgos recorded his final gesture in a poem of the same name, assuring him that, "Your blood is planted in a thousand living signs."

Not by coincidence, two of the eight defendants in the 1936 trials were major poets: Clemente Soto Vélez and Juan Antonio Corretjer.

The orphaned son of landless peasants, Clemente Soto Vélez was born in the mountain town of Lares in 1905. Lares was the site of a historic 1868 revolt against the Spanish, an insurrection still celebrated today on the island every September 23rd as the *Grito de Lares,* or Battlecry of Lares. Though the revolt failed, the symbolism of Lares is deeply embedded in the national psyche, "alive," as Julia de Burgos puts it, "in the great and ferocious Puerto Rican lament / that drips through the lips of the crazy palm trees." (This did not prevent the United States from making the 4th of July an official holiday in Puerto Rico.) Soto Vélez become the living link between nineteenth-century resistance to Spanish colonialism and twentieth-century resistance to North American colonialism.

Soto Vélez co-founded a surrealist literary movement called *La Atalaya de los Dioses,* or *The Watchtower of the Gods,* in 1928.

They made common cause with the Nationalist Party, resulting in a fusion of literary and political movements on the island. As Soto Vélez expressed it, these poets committed themselves to "making revolution from the podium."

Clemente Soto Vélez was a visionary in every sense. He was not only an *independentista,* but a socialist; not only a socialist, but a surrealist who invented his own phonetic alphabet, so no one lacking education could misspell a word. Soto Vélez was also the editor of the Nationalist Party newspaper, called *Armas,* or *Weapons.* The slogan on the masthead read: "Puerto Rican, the independence of Puerto Rico depends on the number of bullets in your belt." This incriminating metaphor was introduced in court; ultimately, Soto Vélez received a six-year sentence.

His first book, *Escalio,* or *Fallow Land,* was published in 1937, the same year the poet was shipped to a federal prison in Atlanta, chained to fellow poet Corretjer for the voyage. *Escalio* ends with a poem called "Solitude." (I co-translated this and the next three poems with Camilo Pérez-Bustillo.)

To fly, alone, to fly
through the skies
of the most incendiary
imagination,
and so, alone, to create,
create the infinite
flight of life.

To think, alone, to think
as all the gathering armies
of creation think,
and so, alone, alone,
alone, to listen
for the original cause
trembling in the light.

To sing, alone, to sing,
as the atoms sing
the will into action,
and so, alone, to sing
as the true awareness
of energy tells it.

Solitude, solitude!
Nimbus of magnetism
balancing all things
within the life-force
that repels it—
solitude, solitude,
heart of life!

Soto Vélez must have experienced this sense of solitude at the Atlanta penitentiary. Forbidden to correspond in any language but English, the poet—who was actually fluent in English—refused on principle to correspond with anyone at all. This spirit of defiance characterized him. When he was released from Atlanta in 1940, on the condition that he not make any more speeches demanding independence, Soto Vélez returned to Puerto Rico and did exactly that. He was immediately re-arrested and served two more years in prison at the penitentiary in Lewisburg, Pennsylvania.

Soto Vélez was a master of paradox. He addresses a political and emotional paradox in the next poem: the fact that he lost his freedom for the love of freedom, that he was walled off from his island for the sake of his island. The poet speaks of himself in the third person, and visualizes himself as a letter of the alphabet, sitting in isolation. This is poem #3 from *The Wooden Horse*.

I met him
living like an h incarcerated in the honey of his bees,
but the bars of honey were bittersweet,
and because
he lost himself
in love with liberation,
and because he did not abandon
his love nor she her lover,
the earth for him is a hurricane of persecuted stars,
since liberation cannot
love anyone
except whoever loves
the earth, with its sun and sky.

Upon his release in 1942, Soto Vélez migrated to New York, where he edited and wrote for the weekly publication *Pueblos*

Hispanos, joined by Juan Antonio Corretjer and Julia de Burgos. Soto Vélez also served as an organizer for radical Congressman Vito Marcantonio and the American Labor Party. He was, above all, a teacher in a community denied access to its own history. Over the years, he mentored countless writers, artists, and activists, myself included.

He became the bridge between the independence movement in Puerto Rico and the Puerto Rican community on the U.S. mainland. Far from being a Hispanophile—a charge sometimes leveled at the Nationalists—the poet connected resistance to North American colonialism in the present with resistance to Spanish colonialism in the past, drawing parallels between the independence movement and the battle of the indigenous Taínos to expel the *conquistadores* from their island.

One such poem retells the fable of Urayoán and Diego Salcedo. By the early 1500s, the Spanish in Puerto Rico had acquired the reputation of being immortal. One *cacique,* or chieftain, by the name of Urayoán decided to test this belief. When a Spanish noble, Diego Salcedo, passed through Urayoán's village and demanded bearers to carry him across a nearby river, the *cacique* instructed the bearers to dump Sr. Salcedo into the river and hold his head under the water to see if he drowned. The bearers conducted their experiment, and returned with their report: *the Spanish die too.* This news triggered a revolt of the Taínos against their Spanish overlords.

Though the uprising was crushed—the Spanish would hang and burn Taínos in groups of thirteen, in honor of Christ and the twelve Apostles—centuries later Clemente Soto Vélez would cite Urayoán's rebellion as an example for the independence movement of his time. The poem is #14 from *The Wooden Horse,* and again the poet refers to himself in the third person.

> I met him
> offering
> an island's tribute to the dare, shimmering
> underwater, that puts the immortal
> to the test, to death
> by drowning, and the water washes up
> this soaked discovery
> like an expired flower;

blunders like claws of contempt drain blood
from the aboriginal tranquility
at the edge of gunpowder and the smoke of humiliation,
but still the longing gleams
and moans in the meditation that drinks
the waters,
so the heart goes on
like an Indian harvesting
stars.

Soto Vélez understood that independence for Puerto Rico was
not the last step, but the first. In 1976, he published an epic work
called *La Tierra Prometida,* or *The Promised Land.* For the poet, the
promised land was not only an independent Puerto Rico, but a
socialist society. His passionately utopian vision saw Fanon's
"wretched of the earth" as the very source of liberation, even
as life-force. This is an excerpt from poem #35, where he expresses
this vision through the simple and delicate use of anaphora:

the promised land
becomes
one
with the hands of the shunned peon . . .
with the hands of the peon
that
thunder in the cartilage of the future
with the hands
of the peon
that
push away
the goldsmiths of plunder
so that
the savored taste of knowledge
is not stolen . . .
with the hands
of the peon
that
are
rainshowers of uncommon poetry
with a fresh breeze of frenzy
perfect
like the violent disturbance of spirit

that
opens
doors wide
to the most
insubordinate sunrises
with the hands
of the peon
that
snatch
the future away
from what it would become . . .
with the hands of the peon
that
plant
sensations of sun
to
become
the nightingale
that does not
sleep
singing
to his existence . . .
with the hands of the peon
that
unionize
gerunds of flurrying verbs . . .
with the hands of the peon
that tame
the two-headed clouds
with the hands of the thinking peon
that
are
the backbones of the word
peon of the word
may the word
become
your servant

By poem's end, the vision is clear: for those who work with
their hands, the key to liberation is literacy. This is a revolution
of and by the word. Perhaps Soto Vélez had in mind the *taba-
queros* of his island, who listened to readers as they rolled cigars

in the factories and therefore made up the most radical sector of the working class.

Clemente Soto Vélez was not only mentor, but friend. My wife and I named our son after him. The poet died in April 1993, and was buried in Lares, the town of his birth. When we visited his grave the following year, we found it unmarked and untended, an apt metaphor for the interment of the independence movement to which he had dedicated his life.

He was the first of many fathers I would lose. I wrote an elegy for Clemente Soto Vélez called, "Hands Without Irons Become Dragonflies." This is the final section:

> Klemente, today we visit your island grave.
> We light a candle for you in chapel
> beneath a Christ executed with beggar's ribs
> and knees lacerated red.
> He is a Puerto Rican Christ.
> In San Juan Bay, a tanker from New Jersey
> bursts a black artery bubbling to the surface,
> so troops along the beach
> in sanitary metallic suits
> scoop the oil clotted into countless bags
> while helicopters scavenge from above.
> Lares now is the property of the state:
> the tamarindo tree
> planted for independence
> in the plaza
> blotched and gray, a rag
> tied around one branch
> like a tourniquet.
>
> At the Lares cemetery nearly a year ago,
> your box sank into a hole
> brimming with rainwater.
> Today the grave we find is desolate clay,
> parched and cracking, a plank marked M75.
> *He is here: burial mound 75,* says the gravedigger.
> So the poet who named us
> suffocates in the anonymity of dirt.
> This is how the bodies of dissenters disappear,
> beneath oceans coated with tanker's blood,
> down to the caves where their voices still drip,

as the authorities guarantee
that this stripped and starving earth is not a grave,
and no one pays the man who carves the stone.
We bury a book with you, pry red flowers
from the trees to embroider the ground,
negotiate the price and labor for a gravestone
as the child with your name races between the tombs.

Klemente, you must be more
than the fragile web of handkerchief
you left behind.
You claimed your true age
was ten thousand light years,
promised that you would someday explode
in atoms, showering down
on us in particles beyond the spectrum
of our sight, visible only to the deities
carved into the boulders by original people
slaughtered five centuries ago.
Now a dragonfly drifts to the forehead
of a vagabond declaiming groggy rebellion
in the plaza, insect-intoxicated,
protesting his own days blindfolded with bars,
his faith louder than an infected mouth.
He says that he remembers you.
On the road to Lares, a horse without a rope
stands before the cars in glowering silence,
infuriating traffic, refusing to turn away
his enormous head. We know
what the drivers must do to pass:
shout *Viva Puerto Rico Libre.*

Hands without irons become dragonflies,
red flowers rain on our hats,
subversive angels flutter like pigeons from a rooftop,
this stripped and starving earth is not a grave.

Juan Antonio Corretjer, imprisoned with Soto Vélez in 1936,
came from Ciales, another mountain town with a revolutionary
history. His father and uncle took part in the *Levantamiento,* or
Uprising, of Ciales in 1898.
Corretjer envisioned a movement for a "liberated homeland"
that was not only working class, but multi-racial, based on a

shared history of labor and exploitation. This was expressed in his epic ode, "Obao-Moin." The translation is my own:

> Glory to those native hands because they worked.
> Glory to those black hands because they worked.
> Glory to those white hands because they worked.
> . . . .
> Glory to the hands that dug the mine.
> Glory to the hands that fed the cattle.
> Glory to the hands that sowed the tobacco, the sugarcane,
>   the coffee.
> Glory to the hands that cut the grasses.
> Glory to the hands that cleared the forests.
> Glory to the hands that rowed the rivers and the channels.
> Glory to the hands that built the roads.
> Glory to the hands that raised the houses.
> Glory to the hands that turned the wheels.
> Glory to the hands that drove the wagons and the cars.
> Glory to the hands that saddled and unsaddled the mules
>   and the horses.
> . . . .
> For them and for their country, Praise! Praise!

Corretjer served as secretary general of the Nationalist Party, and, like his *compañero* Soto Vélez, wrote about the experience of incarceration, finding his voice in the attempt to deprive him of it. This is from "Jail Cell," translated by Roberto Márquez:

> Here is my foot, so small it cannot walk.
> Here, without shadow, is my hand.
> Here are my lips that neither kiss nor talk.
> Here is my voice that dreams but lacks command.
> . . . .
> Here is a face gone pale for lack of sun,
> a heart that beats but beats without a pulse,
> slack, skinless vein, where life's lifeless contained.
>
> Triumph of thought that will not be detained:
> Uplifted in your hand, your heart catapults,
> flowers over the wall, beyond where walls can run.

Corretjer saw the North American occupation of Puerto Rico in the larger context of empire, an empire that consumed everything in its path and would eventually consume itself. From his colonized island and his tiny jail cell, he visualized the eventual self-immolation of U.S. militarism. This is from a later poem called "The Convoy," addressed to his wife Consuelo and translated by Márquez:

> Silence reigns inside the house.
> But on the road
> the military convoy roars its inferno.
>
> Don't wake, my love.
> Let your breathing remain tranquil.
> And your eyes, in the dark,
> blue pursue their sleep.
> Don't wake.
>
> Along the road the convoy's
> thunder. And inside
> my fists the rage.
> Don't move.
> Let your hand lie next to my heart.
>
> The tyrant convoy
> loaded down with guns and worms
> is already heading into the darkness.
> And the darkness has names:
> Jungles, Vietminh, Andes,
> Guevaras . . .
>
> The convoy will collide against that darkness.
>
> Don't wake.
> This is a pause
> for love. Just
> A brief pause.

Corretjer returned to Puerto Rico after his release from prison, and found himself embroiled in another insurgency. In October 1950, there was an armed Nationalist revolt on the island, called the *Grito de Jayuya* after the town where the uprising began. The U.S. Air Force bombed Jayuya, and the rebellion was suppressed within a week. Thousands were rounded up and jailed, including Corretjer and another poet by the name of Francisco Matos Paoli.

Like Clemente Soto Vélez, Francisco Matos Paoli was born in Lares and absorbed the insurgent spirit of that mountain town, rising to a position of leadership in the Nationalist Party. Like Soto Vélez, he would struggle against isolation and silence in prison; unlike his fellow poet, he would lose the struggle. Matos Paoli went mad in solitary confinement, scribbling on the walls. He was ultimately pardoned five years later.

A Christian mystic, Matos Paoli would publish his dreamlike *Song of Madness* in 1962. Here is an excerpt from that long poem, translated by Frances Aparicio:

> Now my feet become dust in the foam.
> And the obscure night
> erases Spring,
> robs me of the full moon of Lares,
> urges the orphan in me
> to abandon the golden bread
> of all constellations.
>
> It so happens that I am mad.
> I return to my mother, the mystic,
> crowned with the poor
> in that sealed, spreading
> penumbra of my village.
> . . . .
> If you want to call me madman,
> I will not oppose the affront.
>
> I know I am the small prisoner,
> the unforgettable vileness of the shadows,
> the conquered yet calm man,
> the slave who forgives the light.
>
> I trust those simple men
> who drift toward
> the iridescent sea.
>
> I sell my skin,
> and . . . who will buy me?
> . . . .
> If you want to dent my sword,
> go ahead.

If you want to steal my poems,
go ahead.

If you want to mistake me for
a crazy John Doe,
go ahead.
. . . .
But you cannot take from me
the delirious feeling that draws me to
the fallen dahlias . . .

There were other forms of punishment. Whenever Corretjer
was not incarcerated, he was pursued by the FBI. They would
have one final confrontation in February, 1984. The poet was
invited to Boston by a coalition of Latino groups. (I was one of
the organizers.) He was slated to speak at a church in the Puerto
Rican community, and on the campus of Harvard University.

On the morning of his first scheduled appearance, nine FBI
agents, guns drawn, surrounded the house where the poet was
staying. They arrested his host, a young musician by the name
of Mariano Viera, and accused him of being somebody else:
Julio Rosado, a fugitive and member of the FALN (*Fuerzas Ar-
madas de Liberación Nacional*), an underground group charged
with numerous bombings in the United States, including one
that resulted in several deaths. We were emphatically not FALN,
but no matter: our office phones were wiretapped. The authorities made no distinction between bard and bomb-thrower.

The FBI established that Viera was not Rosado, but insisted
on holding him anyway, moving their prisoner from one jail to
the next as his lawyers scrambled to find him. Viera turned out
to be claustrophobic, and suffered a breakdown in jail, an eerie
pantomime of Matos Paoli's breakdown years before.

Corretjer was seventy-six years old, with serious coronary
problems. He was shaken by the chaos swirling around him,
yet insisted on speaking at the church and on campus. The
poet's health collapsed in Boston. He returned home to Puerto
Rico, and died less than a year later. His daughter Consuelito
always maintained that the FBI hounded him to death. Mariano
Viera returned to the island, where he was institutionalized.

The organizations that brought Corretjer to Boston, plagued by rumors of an informer in their midst, never worked together again.

If this seems like a description of McCarthyism—decades after Joe McCarthy disappeared from the political landscape— it must be understood that McCarthyism got a head start in Puerto Rico, at least for the advocates of independence. In 1948, two years before McCarthy's notorious claim that the State Department was "infested with communists," *La Ley de la Mordaza*—the Law of the Muzzle—criminalized dissent, making it a felony to "foment, advocate, advise or preach, voluntarily or knowingly, the necessity, desirability or suitability of overthrowing, destroying, or paralyzing the Insular government." Over the years, *independentistas* were jailed, beaten, blacklisted, fired, slandered, spied upon, or simply driven mad. Some felt they had no alternative but to take up arms.

This next poem of mine was written about an artist-friend on the island, and a case of guilt by association:

The Lover of a Subversive Is Also a Subversive
For Vilma Maldonado Reyes

The lover of a subversive
is also a subversive.
The painter's compañero was a conspirator,
revolutionary convicted
to haunt the catacombs of federal prison
for the next half century.
When she painted her canvas
on the beach, the FBI man
squatted behind her
on the sand, muddying his dark gray suit
and kissing his walkie-talkie,
a pallbearer who missed
the funeral train.

The painter who paints a subversive
is also a subversive.
In her portrait of him, she imagines
his long black twist of hair. In her portraits
of herself, she wears a mask
or has no mouth. She must sell the canvases,

for the FBI man lectured solemnly
to the principal at the school
where she once taught.

The woman who grieves for a subversive
is also a subversive.
The FBI man is a pale-skinned apparition
staring in the market.
She could reach for him
and only touch a pillar of ash
where the dark gray suit had been.
 If she hungers to touch her lover,
she must brush her fingers
on moist canvas.

The lover of a subversive
is also a subversive.
When the beach chilled cold,
and the bright stumble of tourists
deserted, she and the FBI man
were left alone with their spying glances,
as he waited calmly
for the sobbing to begin,
and she refused to sob.

In Puerto Rico, as in any colony, there is change without change. In 1952, the island became a U.S. Commonwealth or "Free Associated State," with its own constitution, which was identical in every respect to the United States constitution, and subject to the approval of the U.S. Congress. Puerto Ricans could now exercise a limited form of self-government, including the election of their own governor. The island would be represented in Congress by a non-voting Resident Commissioner, which is still the case.

However, in every way that mattered—politically, militarily, and economically—the United States continued to hold the reins. The status of Puerto Rico had not fundamentally changed. Puerto Ricans kept paying the "Blood Tax," as the draft was called, loading the graves of Utuado with Korean War dead. Nationalists kept going to jail; their last desperate act came in 1954, when four Nationalists opened fire on the House of Representatives, wounding five Congressmen. By the time Puerto Ricans were allowed to vote on their status, in 1967, the independence movement was no longer a threat to the status quo. Decades of repression produced the desired results at the polls.

That repression continued even after the Nationalists were neutralized. In July 1978, two young *independentista* activists were lured to a government radio tower at Cerro Maravilla and executed by a police firing squad. This incident, and the coverup that followed, provoked outrage on the island across the political spectrum. Three years ago, Filiberto Ojeda Ríos, founder of the clandestine militant organization known as the *Macheteros* (or Cane-Cutters), was shot to death by the FBI, again triggering outrage, in no small part because the killing took place on September 23rd: the *Grito de Lares*.

In the United States, many still cling to the illusion that the nation is not, and has never been, an imperial power. Therefore, by definition, Puerto Rico is not a colony. North Americans have internalized the mythology that Puerto Ricans do not desire or deserve self-government. Somewhere beneath lurks the assumption of racial and cultural inferiority.

This is true even on the left. Perhaps the cause of Puerto Rican independence is not sufficiently romantic. To paraphrase Earl Shorris: it's like having dinner with the janitor. There are no peasant armies in the hills, no coffee beans at the café on the corner. There is only the ugliness of poverty, and the colonialism that spawned it.

The same mentality assumes that the Puerto Rican economy must benefit from North American control. Yet the per capita income is less than half that of Mississippi, the poorest state, and the official unemployment rate is in double digits. Puerto Rico is still a colony, not because of North American benevolence, but because the island remains a captive market for U.S. goods, a source of cheap labor for U.S. corporations, and a haven for U.S. military bases.

There is still an independence movement, and there is still protest. In May, 2003, a campaign of civil disobedience forced the Navy to cease war games and live target practice on the inhabited offshore island of Vieques, which the independence movement had loudly condemned since 1941.

The poets, being poets, still won't shut up. The compulsion

to tell this story transcends the borders of geography and language. Jack Agüeros may be a Puerto Rican born in East Harlem, who writes in English; nevertheless, he sums up five centuries of Caribbean history, the frustration of being the world's oldest colony, and the failure to rebel in "Sonnet After Columbus, II." Note the metaphor of paper, representing dollars, contracts, and laws. The reference to the Boston Tea Party and the American Revolution in the last line brings the historical argument full circle.

> We watched the stiff starched sails, the cotton and wood
> On the scale of little boy boats blow onto our shore:
> Our burned out tree canoes were larger and sleeker.
> The Caribbean was quiet, tranquil as ourselves, but
>
> These men were all more hellish than any hurricane,
> And nothing good came after, government after government,
> English, Dutch, Spanish, Yankee, twisting the tongue,
> Jail some, buy some, scare some, dope some, kill plenty.
>
> Do you know the names of the ones in jail or why?
>
> Sailed in our bays and put paper feet on our throats,
> Paper hands in our pockets, papered the trees and land,
> Papered our eyes, and we still wait wondering when.
>
> As for the names of the incarcerated? You and me.
> Charge? Not throwing tea in the bay.

In another sonnet, Agüeros re-imagines the Four Horsemen of the Apocalypse to reflect the reality of Puerto Rican colonialism in "Sonnet for Ambiguous Captivity":

> Captivity, I have taken your white horse. Punctilious
> Death rides it better. Dubious, I try to look you in
> your eye. Are you something like old-time slavery, or
> are you like its clever cousin, colonialism? Are you
> the same as "occupied," like when a bigger bird takes
> over your nest, shits, and you still have to sweep? Or
> when you struggle like the bottom fish snouting in the
> deep cold water and the suck fish goes by scaled in his
> neon colors, living off dividends, thinking banking is
> work? Captivity, you look like Ireland and Puerto Rico!

Four horsemen of the apocalypse, why should anyone fear
your arrival, when you have already grown gray among us
too familiar and so contemptible? And you, Captivity, you

remind me of a working man who has to be his own horse.

The new generation continues to write in this tradition. The
most talented of these young poets, Aracelis Girmay, picks up
the motifs of imprisonment, survival and resistance in her
poem, "Then Sing":

> Now what do you do now
> with a chain around your foot
> or the doors all shut & the phone-wires cut?
> > Make music with the chain,
> > make raw the ankle.
> Locked, locked, locked & thrown away.
> Fall asleep, fall asleep, Houdini, they say,
> we've knocked down all your trees & Albizus.
> . . . .
> > It's prison,
> I know they tell you.
> You will not be anything, you will not even grow.
> Grow anyway.
>
> They will have you believe
> that your body is sick.
> Tell it Live.
>
> When they take away the sunlight,
> even the sunlight, be
> the sunlight.
>
> Let them tell you
> you cannot sing in hell, good man.
> Then sing.

Five hundred and seventeen years of colonialism would be
enough to discourage even the most ardent poet, prophet, or
visionary. Yet, there is reason to hope that Puerto Rico will one
day be an independent and truly democratic nation.

Words have wings. They fly, across time and space, across
oceans and centuries. Sometimes they fly from the dead to the
living. Some years ago in San Juan, I came across a festival orga-

nized by *Claridad,* the island's socialist newspaper. Roy Brown, a singer and guitarist long associated with the cause of independence, was singing the words to a poem by Juan Antonio Corretjer, and thousands were singing along from memory, some in tears, verse after verse that somehow slipped through the keyhole in the jailhouse door and took wing.

Ultimately, for independence to happen, Puerto Ricans must reject the empire's definition of Puerto Ricans and do battle with the colonized self. The poets will be there. Julia de Burgos addressed both the empire and the colonized self when she wrote (in this translation by Agüeros):

> When the multitudes shall run rioting
> leaving behind ashes of burned injustices,
> and with the torch of the seven virtues,
> the multitude will run after the seven sins,
> against you and against everything unjust and inhuman,
> I will be in their midst with the torch in my hand.

Blessed Be the Truth-Tellers

In Praise of Jack Agüeros

On March 20th, 2008, an article by David González appeared on the *New York Times* City Room blog under the headline: *A Puerto Rican Poet's Fight with Alzheimer's.* The poet was Jack Agüeros. González wrote:

> At various points of his career, he has been a community activist, translator, poet and administrator. In Latin America, such people are celebrated for their versatility and value as public intellectuals and defenders of culture. In New York City, such people are often ignored, at least if they come from East Harlem. But those who know Jack treasure his hard-to-pigeonhole passions and accomplishments. More than 100 of his friends and fans gathered on Tuesday night at East Harlem's Julia de Burgos Cultural Arts Center, not just to celebrate his work, but also to help him in a time of need.
>
> Four years ago, he learned he has Alzheimer's. While the disease is still in its early stages, he needs assistance with daily living. That means he needs financial assistance, too, since his application for Medicaid has yet to be approved. As a result, ten poets and writers held a benefit reading to help his children defray the costs of caring for him.
>
> Jack was there, too, chatting with friends and well-wishers. The setting itself was doubly fitting. In 1945, he attended grammar school in the red-brick building, which was then Public School 107. He later immortalized the place in a contrite "Sonnet for Miss Beausoleil," in honor of a teacher whose honor he had offended on a dare. The building is now named for Julia de Burgos, the Puerto Rican poet whose complete works Jack translated in 1996.
>
> "For years, Jack spoke for us," said Martín Espada, a poet

who was twelve years old when he first met Jack. "Tonight, we speak for him."

This essay will speak for Jack Agüeros. He was the first poet I ever knew.

Agüeros was born in East Harlem in 1934. His parents migrated from Puerto Rico. His father, a police officer on the island, came to New York in 1920, laboring in restaurants and factories. His mother arrived in 1931 and worked as a seamstress in the garment district. Agüeros and his family survived on Home Relief during the Depression. He spent four years in the Air Force, where—ironically, given his later life as a dissident—he became a guided missile instructor. After his discharge from the military, he obtained a BA in English from Brooklyn College and an MA in Urban Studies from Occidental College.

Agüeros was a community activist in the 1960s, working with the Henry Street Settlement, the Puerto Rican Community Development Project, and the Wednesday Night Group. In 1968, he was appointed Deputy Commissioner of the Community Development Agency, and immediately stirred up trouble. Agüeros staged a five-day hunger strike in his office to protest mistreatment of the Puerto Rican community by the city administration, stating thirteen conditions to be met before his fast would end. The *New York Times* published a dramatic photograph of Agüeros in his office, his conditions posted on the wall behind him. A stream of city officials and church representatives came to visit, imploring him to terminate the protest. Finally, a letter from Mayor John Lindsay, meeting most of the conditions, persuaded Agüeros to end his hunger strike. He lost twenty pounds in five days. He also demonstrated a gritty integrity that would be reflected in his poems and stories.

From 1977 to 1986, Agüeros was Executive Director of the Museo del Barrio in East Harlem. He invigorated the institution, assembling an impressive collection of carved wooden saints from Puerto Rico, providing space to local Puerto Rican artists and writers, and organizing an annual Three Kings' Day Parade in the barrio, complete with sheep and camels. This endeavor also ended in controversy, as Agüeros was forced out of the Museo by arts administrators at the New York State

Council for the Arts and the Mayor's Office, who saw him as a political threat.

Agüeros wrote a moving account of his childhood called "Halfway to Dick and Jane: A Puerto Rican Pilgrimage" for a collection called *The Immigrant Experience: The Anguish of Becoming American* in 1971. An early landmark anthology of Puerto Rican literature, *Borinquen* (1974), featured several Agüeros poems. However, he did not publish his first book until 1991, when he was fifty-seven years old; he would publish a total of five books in eleven years.

Hanging Loose Press published three collections of poetry by Agüeros: *Correspondence Between the Stonehaulers* (1991); *Sonnets from the Puerto Rican* (1996); and *Lord, Is This a Psalm?* (2002). Curbstone Press published a collection of short fiction by Agüeros, entitled *Dominoes and Other Stories from the Puerto Rican* (1993), and his translations of Puerto Rican poet Julia de Burgos, *Song of the Simple Truth: The Complete Poems* (1997).

Though the work published by Agüeros won two fellowships from the New York Foundation for the Arts, it was ignored by the media and the critical establishment. The journal *Parnassus* was a notable exception. Colette Inez wrote: "With compassion for and indignation at social injustice, he pays homage to the fallen heroes of the barrio, and to those lost in the blur of repetitive work, made invisible or distorted by the lenses of ignorance, fear and bigotry."

Jack Agüeros is one of the few Latino poets who uses the sonnet form, and one of the few writers of the sonnet who engages political themes. (Other contemporaries who write political sonnets include Rafael Campo, Marilyn Nelson, and Marilyn Hacker.)

Agüeros was introduced to the sonnet in high school by his English teacher, Mrs. Finnegan, and cites such influences as Shakespeare, Edna St. Vincent Millay, and Elizabeth Barrett Browning. The title of his second book, *Sonnets From the Puerto Rican,* is a clever play on Browning's *Sonnets From the Portuguese.* Of course, Browning was not Portuguese, and Agüeros is very Puerto Rican. However, these sonnets go well beyond the assertion of cultural identity.

Agüeros takes delight in bending the form. Though each

sonnet is fourteen lines, and most divide themselves into three quatrains and a couplet, he dispenses with iambic pentameter; at times there are only three stanzas, or a concluding "couplet" of only one line. These departures are not haphazard; the poet knows, even loves, the traditional form. Breaking with the form is a declaration of the poet's anarchistic nature, or a reflection of the broken urban world, like a jagged bottle, chronicled by these sonnets. As a bilingual, bicultural poet, Agüeros crosses borders, slipping past the gatekeepers of the King's English and the Queen's Spanish, day and night.

Even when Agüeros departs from the form, he uses it as a device for organizing his ideas or creating dramatic tension. His couplets answer a question posed by the poem, provide a moral, or deliver a punch line. Many of his poems end with a lyrical flourish, a sharp turn, thanks to the poet's strong feel for the couplet.

These are sonnets in impressive variety. There are historical sonnets and journalistic sonnets. There are sonnets evoking landscapes, of the city and elsewhere. There are portraits in sonnet form, mostly of people in the Puerto Rican community. There are sonnets about work and death. There are sonnets of love and the end of love. There are philosophical sonnets. The vision is sweeping, the range of references extraordinary. Often in these poems we see the sonneteer as advocate, demanding respect for his damned and forgotten people and places through the use of a form associated with Shakespeare.

If Public Enemy is "the CNN of the ghetto," then Jack Agüeros is the PBS of the barrio. Thus we have a sonnet cycle about the Happy Land Social Club fire, which killed eighty-seven people in 1990, more than half immigrants from Honduras. The fire was set by the jealous lover of a woman who worked at the club; she escaped unharmed. Agüeros goes beyond the story of Julio González and Lydia Feliciano, confronting the owners of the building for their violations of fire laws (there were no sprinklers and obstructed exits), the courts that slapped the owners with a light fine, and the politicians who failed to keep their promises to the families of the victims.

The most haunting sonnet in this series of five is "Sonnet for the Only Monument Around, October 1994." In a journalistic vein, the poet surveys the scene of the fire more than four years later. He observes that "Smoke stains the cornices / of its few small windows, / hangs over the transom, like / bunting, of its only door." A sign posted by the city announces that a granite monument to the dead will be erected in September, 1994. The penultimate line in the poem offers forceful, immediate evidence to the contrary: "Under my October feet, a ditch full of debris is the only monument."

The poet's photographic eye is in evidence. The ghostly images of the building and the street carry emotional weight. There is a strong sense of place and time; in fact, many Agüeros poems bear an exact date. The poet's sense that the newspapers will never do justice to the "eighty-seven dead dancers" is a major motivation for the creation of these journalistic sonnets. The poet seeks to rescue the dead from oblivion. He understands the difference between a granite monument and a poem, but if the dead cannot have the grand dignity of granite, then they will have the small dignity of a sonnet.

There are other urban landscapes in these sonnets—the number 6 subway train or Tompkins Square Park—but these are not urban pastorals. What draws Agüeros to the landscapes of the city are the human beings that inhabit them. This is especially true when these people are invisible, fading into their environment, for this poet's mission is to make the invisible visible. One such poem is "Sonnet for Heaven Below," documenting a time in New York City when the homeless lived and slept in the subway system by the thousands. `

Agüeros insists that we subvert the traditional definitions of beauty and ugliness, that we gaze upon the "ugly" until it becomes "beautiful." Thus the homeless in this sonnet become fallen angels. The second stanza captures this transformation:

> . . . acid rain fractures their
> Feathers, and french fries and Coca-Cola corrupt
> The color of their skin and make them sing hoarsely.
> The gossamer shoes so perfect for kicking clouds
> Stain and tear on the concrete. . . .

Behind the fantastic imagery is a serious argument: the homeless must be re-imagined. Even the title challenges the reader. "Heaven" is not in the sky above, but "Below," here on earth, because we create our heaven in this place, with an ethos of compassion for fallen angels. Agüeros turns this poem in the last line with characteristic humor: "Mercifully, angels aren't tourists, so they are spared total disdain."

The most striking of the sonnets are dedicated to individual portraiture. These poems clearly demonstrate the unique nexus of form and content in the work of Agüeros. Where else will we find a sonnet for Willie Classen, a Puerto Rican middle-weight boxer killed in the ring? Has there ever been another sonnet for an accused criminal known to the world as "Mad-dog"? If no one else will speak for "Maddog," with the "many multiplying stones / Fast piling across the opening of his life," then the poet, invoking Handel's Messiah, declares: "I stand up." In another character sketch, the poet sees García pushing a clothes rack through the garment district and observes that he gets "no heroic couplet"; of course, Agüeros makes this observation in the couplet of a poem dedicated to García.

In "Sonnet Substantially Like the Words of Fulano Rodríguez One Position Ahead of Me on the Unemployment Line," Agüeros writes:

> It happens to me all the time—business
> Goes up and down but I'm the yo-yo spun
> Into the high speed trick called sleeping
> Such as I am fast standing in this line now.
>
> Maybe I am also a top; they too sleep
> While standing, tightly twirling in place.
> I wish I could step out and listen for
> The sort of music that I must make.
>
> But this is where the state celebrates its sport.
> From cushioned chairs the agents turn your ample
> Time against you through a box of lines.
> Your string is both your leash and lash.
>
> The faster you spin, the stiller you look.
> There's something to learn in that, but what?

"Fulano" is the Spanish equivalent of "John Doe," an Every-man. The toy metaphors stand out: he is a "yo-yo," a "top," toyed with, "spun," "twirling," manipulated by the state, which "celebrates its sport." Standing in line, for Fulano, means being kept in his place; indeed, Puerto Ricans are at the end of the line, economically and politically. He knows that he is more than a case number—"I wish I could step out and listen for / the sort of music that I must make"—but he is defined and dehumanized by the bureaucracy.

Agüeros uses the couplet to articulate a paradox and ask a tough question: "There's something to learn in that, but what?" The poet is bewildered by the spectacle of movement without progress, degradation instead of employment. This is a dignified voice in a situation stripped of dignity, an intelligent voice testifying of intelligence wasted.

However, it would be a mistake to read these sonnets only for their content. There is also craft. If the poet has an eye, he also has an ear, as in "Sonnet for Angelo Monterosa." The poet's friend, Angelo, a small-time crook, has been murdered by shotgun. The poem dedicated to his memory fills to the brim with hard alliteration, underscoring hard realities. He is angry with his dead friend and the murderers, "Killed and killers, killing and dealing dope." There is "blood on the jukebox," the percussive repetition of wasted lives echoed in "the cowbell, the conga and your corpse."

If there are sonnets of advocacy, there are also sonnets of autobiography. If there are portraits, then there are also self-portraits. Agüeros once considered writing a collection of poems about his work history, called *The Book of Jobs.* Though that book never came to fruition, a poem survives called "Sonnet: How I Became a Moving Man." Here the poet's "so-called partners" allow him, on his first day, to move a huge washing machine down four flights of tenement stairs bare-handed, slicing his hands bloody in the process. "What are you going to do now, Kid?," someone asks. His answer, and the response of his co-workers, form the couplet that ends the poem: "'Go get the refrigerator,' I said. 'No,' they said, 'we will / Teach you straps now that you are a man who knows bleeding.'" The bloody hands do not represent some kind of stigmata. Rather, the bleeding becomes a metaphor for the painful knowledge that comes with the years.

No consideration of Agüeros would be complete without a review of the love sonnets. At first glance, there is a superficial resemblance to the love sonnets of Pablo Neruda. Neruda's later sonnets focused on his great love, Matilde Urrutia; likewise, the Agüeros love sonnets focus intensely on one woman, Yolanda Rodríguez. However, a better comparison with Neruda's work exists. The love sonnets of Agüeros, in tone and content, more closely resemble Neruda's early "Song of Despair." There is a sense of anguish over loss, a profound sadness at the transitory nature of love itself.

There is also a fundamental distinction between the young Neruda, twenty years old when he published the "Song of Despair," and the more mature Agüeros, past sixty when he published his love sonnets. Whereas Neruda told his lover, "in you everything sank," Agüeros might well have written, "in *me* everything sank." This poet holds himself responsible for the loss of love. These sonnets call upon the traditional vocabulary of the love sonnet—words like *heart* and *soul* abound—but with a frankness that is very contemporary. They are brutally honest, charged with emotion.

They are also funny. Agüeros avoids the maudlin with his surreal sense of humor. "Sonnet for Me, Your Orbiting Dog," begins: "I am a muzzled dog spun by planet you." In "Sonnet for You, My Moon," the poet mocks his own inability to weep, saying of his tears: "my eyes / are two meticulous waiters incapable of spilling one drop." Elsewhere, he wonders aloud: "How come my bed is empty, even when I am in it?" His self-deprecating humor is visceral; he compares his testicles to "rejectable" prunes. He offers theories of love, tested by experience, like a street-corner philosopher. Love, he has learned, is "a good book borrowed" as if from the library, but "Never say," the poet warns, "'this is my book.'"

The combination of the aging process and the loss of love produces in Agüeros a fascination with death. In the same sonnets where he mourns the end of love, Agüeros speaks of death as a "warm hand" or "welcome as a trip around the world." He sneers at death, "all my teeth in full derision," or becomes "chatty" with the Grim Reaper, since "endless silence" awaits.

Jack Agüeros also writes in a more uncommon form than the

sonnet: the psalm. In these short, spare, often hilarious poems, Agüeros talks to the Lord; whether he actually believes in the Lord is open to question. The psalms divide themselves into poems of praise and poems of heresy. Though the psalms and sonnets have in common the same passion for justice and the same commitment to the Puerto Rican community, the psalms give the poet further license to engage in both celebration and satire.

Though some of these poems may resemble the psalms of Ernesto Cardenal, Neruda again comes to mind. The Agüeros psalms written as hymns of praise closely parallel Neruda's odes, celebrating "ordinary" things and people usually considered unworthy of attention. Neruda wrote an ode to a spoon; Agüeros writes of the pilón, or mortar and pestle, in his kitchen. Neruda wrote odes to the artichoke, the tomato, the onion, the lemon, the watermelon, and garlic; Agüeros writes psalms singing the praises of Puerto Rican delicacies such as rice and beans, tostones, pasteles, bacalao, and coquito. Neruda wrote an ode to the dictionary; Agüeros writes a psalm in defense of Spanish. ("Spanish forever!" he declares—in English.)

The food poems deserve particular attention. The "Psalm for Bacalao" begins by invoking the word itself four times; clearly, the poet is savoring the very flavor of the word *bacalao*—salted and dried codfish. The appreciation of bacalao in the poem goes well beyond its flavor in combination with "green bananas / onions and scrambled eggs." The wonder is that Puerto Ricans have bacalao at all, since the cod "doesn't swim anywhere / near Puerto Rico." The psalm, like the ode, performs a didactic function in the best sense: it educates us about the subject in the process of praising that subject. Since this is a psalm, however, Agüeros makes a transition into the language of miracles: "And Lord / since it's a fish / thank you for letting it fly / to Puerto Rico." This hyperbolic language of the miraculous is often a source of humor in the psalms.

Other psalms in praise of food or drink begin with a light touch, then move into the realm of social commentary. The "Psalm for Coquito"—"a nog with coconut milk and rum," as the poem explains—serves as a springboard for satire on the hypocrisy of the Christmas season. The poem begins with a joke: every other ingredient in coquito, it seems, is rum. Yet, if the poet is a bit tipsy from the coquito, he realizes upon reading the newspaper that the world is drunk on greed, money, and power. He envisions a "dark-skinned family" evicted from "a manger in the South Bronx" and taking up residence at a homeless shelter, "where there were no beds or blankets, / but José got Prozac, / María got Methadone, / and Baby Jesus got scolded for not having a job yet." With this resolution to the poem Agüeros lampoons the Christian Right, who would scorn the infant Jesus and his family for their poverty if they came looking for a manger today.

The food psalms serve another purpose for Agüeros. Since food is a cultural signifier, Agüeros is able to celebrate a Puerto Rican self through these poems. A poem in praise of bacalao is also a poem in praise of Puerto Rican identity. Both the identity and the food continue to be shunned or disrespected; thus, the poem is not only entertaining, but necessary.

Not all the psalms about food involve praise. At least one challenges a God who would allow hunger to exist in the world. "Psalm for the World Restaurant" notes that the "Angel in charge" passes out a strange menu: "One page has no food, / one page has half portions, / one page is all chemical killers." This is a unique way to evoke starvation, malnutrition, and pesticide poisoning, respectively. The mind's eye of the reader might skip over the usual images, so the poet's job is to find a new way, a crazy angle, if need be, to grab the reader's attention. Agüeros uses the Angel to personify capitalist economics: "stuffing his face with raw profits / has destroyed his taste buds." He sardonically urges the Lord to cancel the Angel's "subscription / to *The Harvard Business Review.*"

This is the voice of the poet as heretic. He wrestles with a major philosophical question in these poems: How could a just God tolerate vast human suffering? Instead of leaving that question draped in mid-air for the theologians to contemplate, Agüeros abandons the polite manners of theology and confronts the Lord directly. This confrontation comes with a sharp satirical edge. The "Psalm for Distribution" is a good example:

Lord,
on 8th Street
between 6th Avenue and Broadway
in Greenwich Village
there are enough shoe stores
with enough shoes
to make me wonder
why there are shoeless people
on the earth.

Lord,
You have to fire the Angel
in charge of distribution.

The poem begins by undercutting a basic assumption: maybe the all-seeing God is not all-seeing. The poet presents the injustice obvious to him, but apparently unnoticed by the Deity. The Lord, as the lawyers say, has "actual or constructive knowledge" of the problem: He either knows or should know.

The notion of a dispassionate God turning a blind eye is frightening, yet Agüeros shifts the sobering tone with a punch line. Here the universe is managed by an inept bureaucracy of Angels. The Angel of Distribution can and should be fired by God for his spectacular incompetence. This Angel represents a capitalist system that produces enough resources for everyone, but fails utterly in the fair distribution of those resources. The shoes become, metaphorically, all the basic necessities of life.

The heretical voice in the psalms also mocks the Catholic Church. Agüeros points out that the Pope is fond of a particular car: the Mercedes Benz. (He has five of them, according to the poem.) In poem after poem, the laughter of the poet comes at the expense of the religious hierarchy, from the New Jersey Bishops to the International Theological Commission, which ruled that gays could be sanctified if they were "chaste." Agüeros tugs on the robes of the Lord to ask: "can't you send Jesus / to turn over a few tables / in the temples?"

Yet, the poet insists, he has not lost his faith. An atheist would not write psalms or address a monologue to the Lord. As Agüeros says in "Psalm for My Faith": "Lord, it's not true /

that my faith is cooling. / It's just that people / are saying that candle smoke / has caused cancer in church mice, / and I also worry that candlelight / is too weak to reach your cloud." He is not in the business of libeling religion; he is simply a man with questions.

Agüeros reserves his harshest questions for the state; he has lost faith in that particular human institution. Two strong psalms about police brutality, written many years apart, serve as evidence. The first, "Psalm for Equations," recalls a lethal incident at the Algiers Motel in Detroit in 1967, and concludes furiously: "Lord, you need a new / Angel of Explanations / and a new Angel of Equations / because the dead blacks / far outnumber / the credible police." The second, "Psalm for Amadou Diallo," includes a footnote explaining that Diallo was killed in the South Bronx in 1999 by four police who fired on him forty-one times despite the fact that he was unarmed. This is a model of poetry as the art of the concise, proving that the understatement of outrage can pack an emotional wallop:

> Amadou Diallo
> 1, 2, 3, 4, 5, 6, 7 ??
> Amadou Diallo
> 8, 9, 10, 11, 12, 13, 14,
> Amadou Diallo
> 15, 16, 17, 18, 19, 20, 21,
> Amadou Diallo
> 22, 23, 24, 25, 26, 27, 28,
> Amadou Diallo
> 29, 30, 31, 32, 33, 34, 35,
> Amadou Diallo
> 36, 37, 38, 39, 40, 41,
> Amadou Diallo
> 41,?
> Amadou Diallo
> 41, 41, 41!

On occasion, Agüeros has written poems that are neither sonnets nor psalms. They are fragmentary poems that tell stories in brief or offer thumbnail sketches of people on the block. "Making Him" recalls a junkie, Crazy Benny, who had a disagreement with a crooked dealer going by the equally colorful name of Little Louie. Benny, "with trembling hands," pushed Little Louie off a roof, enforcing an ethical code of the street and becoming, ironically, "a humanitarian of sorts." "And He" sums up the drug addict's dilemma without blame or sentimentality:

> Gorilla in and out
> Of jail, on and off
> Drugs. Thirty-three.
>
> He likes it, and
> He does not like it.

The title poem of the poet's first collection, "Correspondence Between the Stonehaulers," is an outstanding experiment with historical narrative. The six-page poem—by far the longest in his body of work—is an imagined dialogue between a slave in ancient Egypt and another slave in the Inca Empire. Their postcards fly back and forth across centuries. They compare strange creatures (crocodiles and condors). They also compare the proclamations of their rulers: both the Pharoah, Cheops, and the Inca, Manco Capac, decree that "Public works will save us." Both laborers are aware of their exploitation. Nevertheless, both take pride in the raising of their stone monuments.

The poem makes clear that these monuments to kings are, in fact, monuments to the builders. This is a visionary point of view on labor and history, which echoes Neruda's "Macchu Picchu." There is also the echo of Brecht's question: "Who built Thebes of the seven gates?" The poem pays homage on multiple levels: to the historical African and Native roots of Latin American heritage, to the resiliency of those who labor, to their creativity, artistic and otherwise. The poem ends with a tribute to this yearning for expression, and the potential for solidarity among those condemned to silence by their rulers, and by history. The slave of Egypt speaks:

> My friend, one day I will step
> Through the jungle and see the
> Head you carved, and I already love
> It, and one day you will tread the

Soft hot sand and come upon my
Reposing lion-man, smiling.
It is so easy to smile,
So hard to put it on stone.

I cut my finger in your memory.

Beyond his own poetry, Jack Agüeros deserves a great deal of credit for his translations of Julia de Burgos, considered the foremost poet from the island of Puerto Rico. De Burgos poems such as "Río Grande de Loiza" define the Puerto Rican nation, from its natural landscape to its legacy of struggle; others, such as "To Julia de Burgos," anticipate the rise of feminism, asserting the right of women to self-determination: "who governs in me is me." She wrote love poems and political poems, free verse and sonnets, spanning the spectrum.

Julia de Burgos collapsed on an East Harlem street and died in 1953 from complications due to alcoholism. She was not yet forty. (Agüeros notes that Dylan Thomas died of the same causes, at the same age, in the same year and in the same city.) She left behind only two published collections of poetry; a third was published posthumously. The first challenge Agüeros faced was not as a translator, but as an investigator. The early death of Julia de Burgos left countless "lost poems" in its wake.

Agüeros set out to find the "lost poems." He discovered fifty of these uncollected poems in, as he puts it, "obscure magazines, flyers, journals" and elsewhere. One newly discovered poem, "The Voices of the Dead," is an epic piece that ranks with the greatest works of Julia de Burgos, an anti-war poem that still resonates. He even found two poems in English. There will always be more "lost poems"; however, Agüeros has performed a remarkable service in publishing the most complete edition of this poet available either in English or Spanish. *Song of the Simple Truth*, with more than two hundred poems in a bilingual format, represents a literary landmark.

As a translator, Agüeros is rigorous and faithful. He resists the urge to embellish, update, or improve upon the original. He is respectful without being reverential. While he does not impose his own agenda on the poems, there are certain similarities between his poetry and his translations. Like the poems of Agüeros, the translations are clear and direct, playful one moment and profound the next.

Jack Agüeros and Julia de Burgos share a number of characteristics. Both are equally comfortable with lyrics of love or protest. Both favor the independence of Puerto Rico. Both write sonnets. At first glance, it might appear that Agüeros the poet has influenced Agüeros the translator. It is more likely that de Burgos the poet influenced Agüeros the poet, and we are seeing that influence come full circle.

Despite his accomplishments, Jack Agüeros does not rank among the most celebrated of Latino writers. His work is missing from most anthologies, textbooks, and critical surveys of Latino literature. No critic has seen fit to make his work a subject of study. In a community full of neglected writers, the neglect of Agüeros seems particularly unjust.

There are some objective reasons for his lack of recognition. His poetry is published by small presses with limited promotion and distribution. Again, Agüeros did not publish his first book till the age of fifty-seven; now, Alzheimer's disease appears to have closed a window that was opened all too briefly.

Yet Agüeros would appear to be a prime candidate for crossing over into mainstream literary acceptance. He writes sonnets. He addresses a broad range of subjects beyond the Puerto Rican experience. His sense of humor should build bridges with a wider readership. His public readings have been wildly successful with all kinds of audiences.

On the other hand, Agüeros is unabashedly Puerto Rican. In the popular imagination, the Puerto Rican community is illiterate and ignorant. If Puerto Ricans cannot read, the logic goes, then they cannot write, and therefore there are no Puerto Rican writers. The literati are not exempt from these assumptions. The Puerto Rican community has been a significant presence in New York—the literary capital of the country—for more than seventy years, which makes the invisibility of the community's writers all the more inexcusable. (The physical landscape resembles the literary landscape: there is not a single statue of a Puerto Rican in the city of New York.) To date, no Puerto Rican writer in this country has ever won a Pulitzer Prize, or a National Book Award, or a National Book Critics Circle Award, or a MacArthur "genius" grant.

Since Agüeros also writes in a political vein, the violation of literary etiquette is complete. This poet's great offense is not that he takes liberties with the sonnet form, but rather that he demands liberty for those who lack it. Agüeros concentrates on the dignity of his Puerto Rican subjects, rather than their pathology; yet, for the mainstream audience, all too often, pathology *is* authenticity. Hollywood films, for example, focus on the Puerto Rican subject almost exclusively through the lens of criminality.

A more complex question remains: why has Agüeros not received his due in the Puerto Rican literary world? His stubborn independence, his utter uniqueness, may work against him. He defies expectations, even within his own community. He refuses to romanticize self-destruction. David González notes that Agüeros "can talk about those writers (Millay and Dickens) with the same hip voice that betrays his East Harlem roots. That kind of authenticity, however, can confound those who would rather get their inner-city kicks laced with keeping-it-real chaos."

Perhaps Agüeros and his embrace of the sonnet puzzle those who seek more "authentic" Puerto Rican or "urban" expression. The work of Agüeros is hardly assimilationist, yet he also rejects the usual cultural clichés. For Agüeros, being Puerto Rican is necessary but not sufficient; those expecting an exclusive focus on cultural identity will be disappointed. Instead, his work demonstrates that the Puerto Rican experience is more complex than anyone has yet admitted, even more diverse than we have admitted to ourselves.

What ultimately matters is not what Shakespeare called "the bubble reputation," but the work itself, and Jack Agüeros has created a body of work that will last, that will tell future readers the sad, angry, funny truth about being Puerto Rican, and being human, at the end of one century and the beginning of the next.

In March 2008, poets gathered in East Harlem to pay tribute to Jack Agüeros before it was too late, before Alzheimer's could rob him of the capacity to understand their words. David González wrote: "(Lidia Torres), a young poet, took part in Tuesday's benefit, along with other young poets like Aracelis Girmay and Rich Villar. They were joined by older trailblazers like Sandra María Esteves and Julio Marzán. Jack basked in the affection, at times shouting out encouragement or a wisecrack with a flash of his killer smile." Bob Hershon of Hanging Loose Press was there, too. He said to me: "Every time I think of that lively, elegant guy in this situation, it rips me up."

I wrote a poem for the occasion:

Blessed Be the Truth-Tellers
For Jack Agüeros

In the projects of Brooklyn, everyone lied.
My mother used to say:
If somebody starts a fight,
just walk away.
Then somebody would smack
the back of my head
and dance around me in a circle, laughing.

When I was twelve, pus bubbled
on my tonsils, and everyone said:
After the operation, you can have
all the ice cream you want.
I bragged about the deal;
no longer would I chase the ice cream truck
down the street, panting at the bells
to catch Johnny the ice cream man,
who allegedly sold heroin the color of vanilla
from the same window.

Then Jack the Truth-Teller visited the projects,
Jack who herded real camels and sheep
through the snow of East Harlem every Three Kings' Day,
Jack who wrote sonnets of the jail cell
and the racetrack and the boxing ring,
Jack who crossed his arms in a hunger strike
until the mayor hired more Puerto Ricans.

And Jack said:
You gonna get your tonsils out?
Ay bendito cuchifrito Puerto Rico.
That's gonna hurt.

I was etherized,
then woke up on the ward
heaving black water onto white sheets.
A man poking through his hospital gown
leaned over me and sneered:
You think you got it tough? Look at this!
and showed me the cauliflower tumor
behind his ear. I heaved up black water again.

The ice cream burned.
Vanilla was a snowball spiked with bits of glass.
My throat was red as a tunnel on fire
after the head-on collision of two gasoline trucks.

This is how I learned to trust
the poets and shepherds of East Harlem.
Blessed be the Truth-Tellers,
for they shall have all the ice cream they want.

I've Known Rivers

Speaking of the Unspoken Places in Poetry

To some poets, a lake is exactly that, a body of water, a place for bird-watching or contemplation of nature's mysteries.

To Everett Hoagland, a lake is something more. He stands at the edge of Lake Champlain, and wonders, "who walked in, fell in, jumped in, went / under to lake bed long ago." He reports: "Something unseen splashed." His poetic imagination takes him below the surface of the water, beyond whatever we see or want to see, to envision suffering humanity.

There are "unspoken" places all around us, places we never see, or see but do not see. There are hidden histories, haunted landscapes, forgotten graves, secret worlds surrounded by high walls, places of pilgrimage where pilgrimage is impossible. Sometimes, these places are "unspoken" because the unspeakable happened or continues to happen there; sometimes, because the human beings dwelling in the land of the unspeakable find a way to resist, and their example is dangerous.

Speaking of the unspoken places means speaking of the people who live and die in those places. These are people and places condemned to silence, and so they become the provinces of poetry. The poet must speak, or enable other voices to speak through the poems. Indeed, poets continue to speak of such places in terms of history and mythology, memory and redemption. They pose difficult questions: Who benefits from silence and forgetting? Who benefits from speaking and remembering? How do we make the invisible visible? How do we sing of the world buried beneath us? How do we soak up the ghosts through the soles of our feet?

On October 31, 1943, Pablo Neruda climbed on horseback

through the Andes to the ruins of an Inca city called Macchu Picchu. Here there is no Spanish architecture, or destruction of indigenous architecture. As Neruda translator and critic John Felstiner observes, "Because of its inaccessibility, the conquistadors never got to Macchu Picchu and may not have known about it." It a place "arrested in time," a miraculous sight: "The city itself gives you a feeling of physical improbability. Perched on a saddle between two pinnacles two thousand feet above the Urubamba (River), its walls, towers, stairways and roofless houses seem to be clinging organically onto the grassy ridge . . . Wherever you go in the city you are moving up or down." Yet, "As for the builders, no trace remains of their dwellings or those of the various artisans and farmers who supported such a community."

Neruda wrote *The Heights of Macchu Picchu* in September 1945, a long poem divided into twelve Cantos. As might be expected, he praises the power of the city and the mountains. However, in Canto X there is a radical turnabout. With the question, "Man, where was he?" Neruda confronts Macchu Picchu. He becomes aware of human suffering at this sacred place. The poet asks: "Macchu Picchu, did you lift / stone upon stone on a groundwork of rags?" To build the city thousands of slaves must have labored for years to drag huge stones two thousand feet above the Urubamba without the use of the wheel. Neruda wrestles with the paradox that such magnificence is built upon such suffering. He demands of Macchu Picchu: "Give me back the slave you buried here!"

Most poets would write in praise of Macchu Picchu's splendor, and leave it at that. Instead, according to René de Costa, "The soul of the poet is united not with nature or with God, as in traditional mystic poetry, but with the continent and its past history." This is a different kind of communion, not mystic, but militant.

The poem takes one more turn in the twelfth and final Canto. Standing at the heights of Macchu Picchu, Neruda speaks to and for the dead:

> Look at me from the depths of the earth,
> tiller of fields, weaver, reticent shepherd,
> groom of totemic guanacos,
> mason high on your treacherous scaffolding,

iceman of Andean tears,
jeweler with crushed fingers,
farmer anxious among his seedlings,
potter wasted among his clays—
bring to the cup of this new life
your ancient buried sorrows.
. . . .
Point out to me the rock on which you stumbled,
the wood they used to crucify your body.
Strike the old flints
to kindle ancient lamps, light up the whips
glued to your wounds throughout the centuries
and light the axes gleaming with your blood.

I come to speak for your dead mouths.

The translation is by Nathaniel Tarn. As de Costa says, the poet "calls out to the continent's dead, asking them to speak through him." Neruda will "speak with a voice of Biblical authority for all the people of the Américas." In the epiphanic declaration, "I come to speak for your dead mouths," the poet reveals the synthesis between craft and commitment, poetry and politics. This is why he writes, and why he lives. In Canto XII, Felstiner notes, Neruda wants the flesh and blood of the dead "transfused into him. Lives that were stifled in the mother of stone can rise to be born through him."

Some places, like Macchu Picchu, are forgotten through negligence, while other places are forgotten with great deliberation. Poet Sterling Brown served as the "Negro editor" of the Federal Writers' Project during the 1930s. According to Mark Sanders, Brown wrote "Remembering Nat Turner" in "direct response to the disillusioning experience with the Federal Writers' Project. Brown's chief assignment at the Project was to oversee the recovery of African-American history . . . But Brown repeatedly encountered, from whites and blacks, apathy and ignorance of history and its possibilities."

Nat Turner was a Black preacher who led a slave revolt in Southampton County, Virginia in 1831, killing fifty-five whites at various plantations. Turner was caught and hanged with his fellow insurgents. (Turner was also decapitated, quartered, and skinned.) "Remembering Nat Turner" is ironically titled; in fact, it's all about forgetting Nat Turner.

The Black sharecroppers in Cross Keys, where the rebellion began, have "only the faintest recollections": "So he fought to be free. Well. You doan say." An elderly white woman misremembers maliciously:

> She cackled as she told how they riddled Nat with bullets
> (Nat was tried and hanged at Courtland, ten miles away).
> She wanted to know why folks would come miles
> Just to ask about an old nigger fool.

Worse still is the truth she tells:

> We had a sign post here with printing on it,
> But it rotted in the hole, and thar it lays,
> And the nigger tenants split the marker for kindling.

The Black tenants are not only ignorant of their own history; they build a fire out of it. Their immediate needs override any knowledge of themselves or the possibility of changing their own lives. They can't learn their history from a sign they can't read. As Sanders observes, "they destroy the artifacts that hold the key to both past and future."

Meanwhile, the searchers depart, finding no trace of Nat Turner and his army, nowhere to lay their hands:

> A watery moon was high in the cloud-filled heavens,
> The same moon he dreaded a hundred years ago.
> The tree they hanged Nat on is long gone to ashes,
> The trees he dodged behind have rotted in the swamps.
> . . . .
> We remember the poster rotted through and falling,
> The marker split for kindling a kitchen fire.

The split marker is a metaphor for the obliteration of history and memory, burning away, dissolving in ash and swamp. Yet, the very obliteration of Nat Turner argues for the importance of his reclamation by the poet. This is why poems like "Remembering Nat Turner" are necessary: so that the truth of a place cannot be erased simply by changing the face of the landscape.

If Neruda was haunted by stone, and Brown was haunted by fire, there are other poets who are haunted by water. History and memory are not only buried in the earth; they are carried away by rivers. Nevertheless, there are voices rising from the current.

Claribel Alegría's poem "The Rivers" has a dreamlike, surreal quality, yet the recurrent image of the rivers carrying away the dead is not the product of magical realism. On May 14, 1980, there was a massacre at the Sumpul River in El Salvador, where the Salvadoran military slaughtered six hundred peasants trying to flee across the river into Honduras. This is never mentioned explicitly in the poem; instead, the Sumpul Massacre is the poet's point of departure, as translated by Alegría's husband, Darwin Flakoll:

> the rivers are coffins
> crystalline flasks
> cradling their dead
> escorting them
> between their wide banks
> the dead sail down
> and the sea receives them
> and they revive.

In the rivers "boiling with corpses" the poet has found a metaphor to depict the collective memory of El Salvador after years of brutal repression that left 70,000 dead in a country the size of Massachusetts. This accounts for the grief and compassion of the rivers; they "cradle" their dead. If the rivers are obliged to bear the dead in a mass funeral procession, they will become magnificent coffins, "crystalline flasks." But this is not an elegy per se. In a surprising turn, the rivers bring the dead to the sea, where "they revive." In the water of communal memory there exists the possibility of redemption and healing. There is desecration, but there is also purification.

Carl Sandburg, himself a veteran of the Spanish-American War, recalls the battlefields of the world in "Grass":

> Pile the bodies high at Austerlitz and Waterloo.
> Shovel them under and let me work—
>   I am the grass; I cover all.

And pile them high at Gettysburg
And pile them high at Ypres and Verdun.
Shovel them under and let me work.
Two years, ten years, and passengers ask the conductor:
What place is this?
Where are we now?

I am the grass.
Let me work.

These few words capture the endless cycles of war made possible by historical amnesia. The proof of this amnesia is evident in the litany of the poem itself. We all recognize the names "Gettysburg" and "Waterloo." The other names are less familiar to our contemporary eyes and ears. Verdun is a city in France, the site of a battle during the First World War that lasted for ten months. Total casualties: Over 900,000. Ypres is a city in Belgium, the site of three battles during the Great War. Austerlitz is a town in Czechoslovakia, the site of a major battle during the Napoleonic Wars. The poem then poses a question that resonates on multiple levels: "Where are we now?" The answer echoes back: *Iraq*.

This poem can be read as a response to Whitman's question in "Song of Myself": "What is the grass?" The voice of the grass here is so indifferent to the piles of bodies that it might as well be the voice of an uncaring God. There is no doubt, however, that the voice bears witness to a fundamental truth. Visit Gettysburg, and another truth of the poem reveals itself: the grass is beautiful. The grass covers all, and the place is once again idyllic, as if the generals choose their battlefields the same way most of us choose the perfect spot for a picnic. The grass becomes a metaphor for the seductiveness of forgetting.

Any survey of poems that speak of hidden or forgotten places must account for the poetry arising from incarceration. The empathy of Whitman for prisoners points the way: "Not a man walks handcuffed to the jail, but I am handcuffed / to him and walk by his side." This poetry is especially relevant given the epidemic of incarceration in the United States today. The media tend to demonize those behind the walls—the comforting personification of criminality in a cage—but beyond the symbolism there is invisibility and silence. Poetry humanizes, giving the prisoner a face and a voice.

Nâzim Hikmet spent seventeen years in prison for his political activity with the Communist Party in Turkey. In particular, he was charged with sedition when cadets at the naval academy were caught reading his poems. In May, 1949, locked up in Bursa Prison, he wrote "Some Advice to Those Who Will Serve Time in Prison." The poem has an urgency that draws us in, but the poet also employs several strategies to keep us there. There is, first of all, his strategy of addressing the audience. As Ed Hirsch observes of this poem: "Consider yourself addressed if you're going to be spending time in prison for political reasons." For the rest of us, there is an experience akin to eavesdropping. Instinctively, we lean closer to catch every word. There is another strategy at work: the poet springs at us from strange and surprising angles. There is no mention of the warden, guards, other inmates, bars on the windows, steel doors or the prison yard. Instead, this is a poem about the *emotional landscape* of the dissenter. The advice, by poem's end, is not only about surviving imprisonment, but about our own emotional landscapes, whatever they may be. This is the end of the poem, translated by Randy Blasing and Mutlu Konuk:

> And who knows,
> the woman you love may stop loving you.
> Don't say it's no big thing:
> it's like the snapping of a green branch
>   to the man inside.
> To think of roses and gardens inside is bad,
> to think of seas and mountains is good.
> Read and write without rest,
> and I also advise weaving
> and making mirrors.
> I mean, it's not that you can't pass
>   ten or fifteen years inside
>   and more—
>   you can,
>   as long as the jewel
>   on the left side of your chest doesn't lose its luster!

Hirsch says of Hikmet and his emotions:

He knows, for example, one can't afford to give in to desolation. He is against brooding about enclosed spaces, even beautiful ones like gardens, but supports dreaming of wild open spaces, like seas and mountains. He understands too well the temptations of sadness, the dangers of indifference, the healing power of laughter . . . So many modern and contemporary poets are terrified of deep feeling, of seeming undefended and "sentimental" . . . Many write as if it were desirable to refine out the emotional registers of the lyric. We live in a cool age. But I invoke Hikmet precisely for his emotional excesses, for writing an oracular human-sized poetry, for his toughness and unblushing sentiment, for calling the heart a jewel that should never lose its luster.

Etheridge Knight, wounded in the Korean War, was treated with morphine and became an addict. He was ultimately convicted of armed robbery and spent six years in prison, where he began to write. His most celebrated poem—possibly the most celebrated poem about prison life in this country—is called "Hard Rock Returns to Prison from the Hospital for the Criminal Insane."

Hard Rock is a rebel and a hero to his fellow inmates. They recall his legendary exploits, such as the time he smacked a guard with his dinner tray, and "the jewel of a myth that Hard Rock had once bit / a screw on the thumb and poisoned him with syphilitic spit." The authorities finally send Hard Rock to a mental hospital, and he returns lobotomized, "his eyes empty like knot holes in a fence." The poet goes on:

And even after we discovered that it took Hard Rock
Exactly 3 minutes to tell you his first name,
We told ourselves that he had just wised up,
Was being cool; but we could not fool ourselves for long,
And we turned away, our eyes on the ground. Crushed.
He had been our Destroyer, the doer of things
We dreamed of doing but could not bring ourselves to do.

Of "Hard Rock," Yusef Komunyakaa writes:

Knight knows that people in such a psychological clench need heroes of mythic proportions to fight their real and imaginary battles. Hard Rock is one that they, and Knight, have claimed. He has a history of standing up to adversaries and symbols of authority, a figure of folkloric stature . . . This hero doesn't wear a white hat. He is crude, brute-looking, unsophisticated, but also noble. In order for him to belong to a group he must sacrifice himself; thus, he's misused by this fraternity of black victims. Also, one knows, like Hard Rock what the collective "we" has been reduced to—that only savagery equals survival in such a hellhole. The situation has invented Hard Rock.

Etheridge Knight demonstrates the proposition that the people who inhabit the unspoken places are not only subjects, but poets themselves. They have moral and literary authority to speak. In fact, there is probably a higher percentage of poets per capita in the prison system than in the educational system. Poets who survive and emerge from the prison system will often say, with all solemnity, that poetry saved their lives, as melodramatic as that statement might seem in the academic world.

There is yet another perspective: those who work behind the walls have their point of view. Theodore Deppe served as a psychiatric nurse working with disturbed adolescents at a hospital in Willimantic, Connecticut. This poem is simply called, "Admission, Children's Unit":

> She said her son set fire to his own room,
> she'd found him fanning it with a comic, and what
> should she have done? Her red hair
> was pulled back in a braid, she tugged at its flames,
> and what she'd done, it turns out, was hold her son
> so her boyfriend could burn him with cigarettes.
> The details didn't, of course, come out at first,
> but I sensed them. The boy's refusal to take off his shirt.
> His letting me, finally, lift it to his shoulders
> and examine the six wounds, raised, ashy, second
> or third degree, arranged in a cross.
> . . . .
> I'd like to say all this happened when I first started
> to work as a nurse, before I'd learned not to judge

the parents, but this was last week, the mother was crying,
I thought of handing her a box of tissues, and didn't.
. . . .
Sullen and wordless, the boy got up, brought his mother
the scented, blue Kleenex from my desk,
pressed his head into her side. Bunching
the bottom of her sweatshirt in both hands,
he anchored himself to her. Glared at me.
It took four of us to pry him from his mother's arms.

There is a current of controlled anger that runs through the poem, channeled and directed rather than spilling over. Thus, the poem mirrors the controlled anger of the poet at the very moment that this encounter occurred. The poem succeeds, not simply because of the shocking tale it tells, but because the poem pivots like a skier down a slope, building momentum and leaving our expectations sprawled in its wake. First comes the revelation of the burns in the shape of a cross; then the refusal of the nurse (that is, the poet) to hand over a box of tissues, in a small gesture of hostility; then the son bringing his mother the tissues, signaling his loyalty; then the final, devastating struggle. The victim does not want help, despises his protector, and fiercely loves a person who may ultimately kill him.

The poem raises a basic question: Why was it written? Unlike Neruda, Hughes, Sandburg, or Hikmet, Ted Deppe is not famous. He has published four slim collections of poetry with small presses. His audience is small. When he wrote this poem, he had no expectations that it would be published or read at all, or that the poem could possibly change the boy's situation for the better. Why does a psychiatric nurse write a poem?

"Admission, Children's Unit" represents the fact that we speak of the unspoken places because *we have to,* regardless of consequences, that we are driven to create a record of human suffering—and resistance to suffering—without the luxury of measuring our impact on the world, which cannot be quantified. We write such poems because there is an ethical, even physical compulsion to write them.

There are, to be sure, consequences for the failure to speak of the unspoken places. Witness the public discourse in this country on the legitimacy of torture. The poet Roque Dalton had something to say from the other side of that particular wall.

Dalton, according to Eduardo Galeano, "twice escaped death up against the wall" in El Salvador: "Once he was saved because the government fell; the second time because the wall itself fell, thanks to an opportune earthquake. He also escaped from the torturers, who left him in bad shape but alive, and from the police, who chased him with blazing guns." Finally, he was assassinated in 1975 by an extreme faction on his own side. As Galeano puts it: "This bullet, the only one that could find Roque, had to come from right beside him." Dalton would have appreciated the irony. His poem about the unspeakable is called, "The Certainty," translated by Jack Hirschman.

Two torturers play a guessing game with their prisoner: "If you guess which one of us / has a glass eye, you'll be spared torture." The prisoner gets it right—"His. His right eye is glass"—and the amazed guards want to know:

> "But how did
> you guess? All your buddies missed because the eye is
> American, that is, perfect." "Very simple," said the prisoner,
> feeling he was going to faint again, "it was the only eye that
> looked at me without hatred."

> Of course they continued torturing him.

One "certainty" of this poem is that the poet never stops being a poet, even when writing about torture. Roque Dalton speaks in metaphor. The glass eye is a representation of U.S. foreign policy in El Salvador. The eye is apparently "perfect," and indeed the rhetoric of U.S. foreign policy invokes democratic principles as well as the desire for peace. But the eye is glass, a gleaming fraud. Ultimately, the eye is blind. The United States once funded the Salvadoran military at a rate of more than one and a half million dollars per day, yet the taxpayers and the bureaucrats never saw the torture chamber.

The poem has the quality of a perverse fable, with a political moral. The guards pose a riddle; the prisoner answers correctly, and loses anyway. Perhaps Dalton's moral is this: Don't play the game with this regime. Name "hatred" for what it is. Dalton adopts a different survival strategy than Nâzim Hikmet; he stays human through stubborn defiance.

A glimpse into the jail cell where torture takes place is relatively rare; so, too, is the glimpse into the doorway of the fine house where torture has been sanctioned. In "The Colonel," a poem about her experience in El Salvador, Carolyn Forché brings us through that doorway. This poem is a prime example of what Forché calls "the poetry of witness," influenced by the Latin American tradition of the "testimonio." Here Forché is acting as a poet-spy—and she gets caught, escalating the tension of the scene.

The poem begins with a statement of immediacy: "What you have heard is true." Forché then establishes a sense of place in two ways. We see images of privilege: "rack of lamb, good wine, a gold bell." We also see images of the barriers protecting privilege: "Broken bottles were embedded in the walls around the house to / scoop the kneecaps from a man's legs." The poem lifts us safely over those broken bottles. The poet becomes our guide to a secret place, where the euphemistic language of power asserts itself in such phrases as "how difficult it had become to govern," the rationalization for whatever happens in that *other* secret place, the jail cell of Roque Dalton.

But the guide is powerless when her host, the colonel, decides to demonstrate his ultimate authority at the dinner table:

> The colonel returned with a sack used to bring groceries
> home. He spilled many human ears on the table. They were
>   like
> dried peach halves. There is no other way to say this.

The sack of ears has metaphorical power—a startling representation of silence imposed by brutality—but they are also real ears. This turn in the poem is followed by one more dramatic development: the colonel, obviously a dangerous man, knows who the poet is and where her sympathies lie: "As for the rights of anyone, tell your people they can go fuck themselves." The implication here is that she or her "people" could be imperiled. The colonel's final declaration—"Something for your poetry, no?"—could be read as a dare, or as a statement that his power and privilege insulate him from punishment or reprisal. It doesn't matter what she writes. Of course, the colonel was wrong. The poem gained a good deal of attention in the United States and helped to raise awareness about repression in El Salvador. (According to Forché, the colonel is dead now.)

There are many Latino writers and activists who insist that the border between México and the United States is a nation unto itself, with its own culture and history. If so, then this is truly an unspoken place, a shadow country. In 1987, the United States government attempted to prevent Demetria Martínez from speaking of this unspoken place.

Martínez, a Chicana poet, novelist, and journalist from Albuquerque, was active in the sanctuary movement during the 1980s that provided political asylum for refugees from Central America. In her capacity as a writer, she traveled in the company of two pregnant Salvadoran women as they crossed the border into the United States. She wrote a poem about the encounter called "Nativity: For Two Salvadoran Women, 1986–1987." In 1987, Martínez was indicted for allegedly smuggling "illegal aliens" across the border. She faced twenty five years in prison and more than a million dollars in fines. The poem was introduced as evidence against her, to show that she indeed traveled with the refugees, though the existence of the poem supported her contention that she was acting as a writer. She was acquitted on First Amendment grounds in 1988. However, her treatment may help to explain why so many unspoken places remain unspoken.

Martínez wrote "Nativity" to protest the criminalization of the immigrant, to argue that the phrase *illegal immigrant* is an oxymoron in a nation of immigrants. In return, her dissent was criminalized, since the best way to circumvent the First Amendment and punish dissent is to call the dissenter a criminal and charge her with a crime.

The journalistic sensibility of the poem is clear. The elements of who, what, and where are present in the opening lines:

> Your eyes, large as Canada, welcome
> this stranger.
> We meet in a Juárez train station

where you sat hours,
your offspring blooming in you
like cactus fruit,
dresses stained where breasts leak,
panties in purses tagged
"Hecho en El Salvador,"
your belts like equators
mark north from south,
borders I cannot cross,
for I am an American reporter,
pen and notebook, the tools
of my tribe, distance us . . .

The poem transcends journalism as it mythologizes this place and people. The title itself mythologizes: "Nativity." The children are due in December; the birth of these children represents hope for a people to survive; they will be born in the "manger" of this society.

The poet-reporter watches a car taking the two Salvadoran women to their destiny, "a canoe hanging over the windshield / like the beak of an eagle, / babies turning in your wombs, / summoned to Bélen to be born." The last line of the poem relies on the double meaning of "Belén" in Spanish: both "Bethlehem" and "chaos." The children are summoned to a mythological destiny, but also to a chaotic and dangerous world. The line echoes Yeats: "slouching towards Bethlehem to be born."

These immigrants cross the border into unspoken places: the fields and labor camps of this country. From this world, where illiteracy is the rule, came Chicano poet Gary Soto. A former farmworker in the San Joaquín Valley, Soto published *The Elements of San Joaquín* in 1977. It was almost as if Tom Joad had written *The Grapes of Wrath*. "A Red Palm," a later poem, establishes its central metaphors of dehumanization in the first two stanzas:

You're in this dream of cotton plants.
You raise a hoe, swing, and the first weeds
Fall with a sigh. You take another step,
Chop, and the sigh comes again,
Until you yourself are breathing that way
With each step, a sigh that will follow you into town.

That's hours later. The sun is a red blister
Coming up in your palm. Your back is strong,
Young, not yet the broken chair
In an abandoned school of dry spiders.
Dust settles on your forehead, dirt
Smiles under each fingernail.

The person becomes the place, and the place becomes the person. The "weeds / fall with a sigh," until "you yourself are breathing that way," "a sigh that will follow you into town." Later that night, "you walk with a sigh of cotton plants." The farmworker is both chopping and chopped. He dissolves into the cotton, no more human than the crop and the dirt, which "smiles under each fingernail," as human as he is. "The sun is a red blister" in the palm; by the end of the poem, the "red sun" is "the sore light you see when you first stir in bed," an image that implies that the farmworker and the sun will rise together for another day in the fields. The comparison of the blister and the sun is significant. In farmworker literature, the sun is a malevolent presence, not a harbinger of hope or a bringer of life.

The red palm is a brand, an identifying mark, reminiscent of the stigmata. All the farmworker owns is the labor of his hands. That labor buys rest from labor, but the respite is painfully brief. The lights are on: "That costs money, yellow light / In the kitchen. That's thirty steps, / You say to your hands." The hands twitch. There may be rest, but there is no peace.

Diana García was born in a migrant labor camp: Camp CPC, owned by the California Packing Corporation in the San Joaquín Valley. Like Etheridge Knight, García demonstrates the presence of poets in the unspoken places. She writes a visceral poetry, from the perspective of one who escaped. There is a flicker of imagination in the emulation of a beloved movie star—the seed of poetry, perhaps.

When living was a labor camp called Montgomery

you joined the family each summer to sort dried figs.
From Santa María to Gilroy, Brawley to Stockton, you settled
in rows of red cabins hidden behind the orchards.

You recall how the red cabin stain came off on your fingers,
a stain you pressed to your cheeks so you looked like
Dolores del Río, the famous Mexican actress.
. . . .
You catch the stench of rotting figs, of too-full outhouses.
The nose closes off. You feel how hot it was to sleep, two
to a mattress, the only other room a kitchen.

You thought your arms thickened long ago lugging trays of
    figs.
You thought you had peasant ankles. You thought you could
    die
in the camp and no one would know your smell.

We return, full circle, to water.

Langston Hughes published "The Negro Speaks of Rivers" at
the age of nineteen. Biographer Arnold Rampersad says that the
poem came to Hughes as he was riding a train that crossed the
Mississippi over a long bridge. In the poet's words:

> I began to think what that river, the old Mississippi, had
> meant to Negroes in the past—how to be sold down the river
> was the worst fate that could overtake a slave in bondage.
> Then I remembered reading how Abraham Lincoln had
> made a trip down the Mississippi on a raft, and how he had
> seen slavery at its worst, and had decided within himself that
> it should be removed from American life. Then I began to
> think of other rivers in our past—the Congo, and the Niger,
> and the Nile in Africa—and the thought came back to me:
> "I've known rivers," and I put it down on the back of an en-
> velope I had in my pocket . . .

Fifteen minutes later, one of the key poems of the African-
American tradition was born:

> I bathed in the Euphrates when dawns were young.
> I built my hut near the Congo and it lulled me to sleep.
> I looked upon the Nile and raised the pyramids above it.
> I heard the singing of the Mississippi when Abe Lincoln
>   went down to New Orleans, and I've seen its muddy
>   bosom turn all golden in the sunset.
>
> I've known rivers:
> Ancient, dusky rivers.
>
> My soul has grown deep like the rivers.

Hughes, like Neruda and Sandburg, was a disciple of Whitman, reflected here by the sweeping scope of his vision. But the vision belongs to Hughes—he, too, sings America. Rampersad says:

> The death wish, benign but suffusing, of its images of rivers older than human blood, of souls grown deep as these rivers, gives way steadily to an altering, ennobling vision whose final effect gleams in the evocation of the Mississippi's 'muddy bosom' turning at last "all golden in the sunset." Personal anguish has been alchemized by the poet into a gracious meditation on race, whose despised ('muddy') culture and history, irradiated by the poet's vision, changes within the poem from mud into gold.

Ultimately, this is a poem about all rivers, all submerged histories, all unspoken places, and the poets who alchemize the mud into gold.

A Branch on the Tree of Whitman
Martín Espada on the 150th Anniversary of
Leaves of Grass

An Interview with Edward Carvalho
July 4th, 2005, Castle Hill Center for the Arts, Truro, Massachusetts

Carvalho: What initially drew you to Whitman as a poet? How did you first discover him? Were you inspired more by a stylistic interest in his aesthetic, or through the attention he afforded the dispossessed? What are the aspects of his voice that have found their way into your own work?

Espada: Let's take these one at a time, starting with what initially drew me to Whitman. I would say, first of all, that when I first encountered Whitman I wasn't ready for him. I wasn't ready, in part, because nobody taught Whitman to me. I did not get any Whitman in high school; I did not get any Whitman in college. We're talking about the 1970s now. All too often Whitman was, and I think to some extent still is, quietly censored or sanitized in this country. It's ironic because, at the same time, he has gained a reputation as one of our great poets, and certainly the founder of so much of what we call "poetry" today. Yet, in a tangible way, we're not ready for Whitman as a society. We're still not ready for his message of radical egalitarianism; we're not ready for his expressions of compassion for everyone. Many of us are not ready for his sexuality.

Therefore, I had to come to Whitman on my own and very slowly. When I did, I realized something: I had been reading Whitman all along without knowing it. His influence is that pervasive. You can read a poet like Allen Ginsberg or, for that matter, Pablo Neruda and not realize you're reading Whitman.

You're not aware that you are actually looking at *Leaves of Grass* when you're reading *Canto General* or *Howl*. I had come to other poets in Whitman's lineage, in the Whitman tradition, before I came to him. When I finally came to him with that understanding, that he was everywhere, I had a deeper appreciation for him.

I remember walking around with a copy of *Leaves of Grass* everywhere I went. I'd carry it with me. I would underline and star certain lines or passages. I would read him out loud to anybody who would listen, and some who wouldn't listen. At a certain point I began to look at *Leaves of Grass* as almost Biblical in its resonance, in its impact on how I saw the world. This wasn't something that happened overnight; it took me a while to figure out how important this voice was to me.

There is a particular element of Whitman that most appeals to me, and that's Whitman the advocate. You find indications of Whitman the advocate throughout his work: that motif in "Song of Myself" of identification with the damned. He takes it upon himself to become a voice for the voiceless. He declares his intentions, which sets him apart from most other poets. He says "this is what I'm going to do," and then he does it. Whitman is a teacher; he's fully aware of the instruction he's giving and is unembarrassed about giving it. This is refreshing, actually, when you consider how many poets have a hidden agenda. Many poets don't come out and say what's on their minds. There's never any doubt to me that Whitman is saying what he's saying, and that he means what he means.

But that Whitman—Whitman the advocate—has had the greatest effect on me and on other poets. Neruda again comes to mind. Neruda expressly took on the role of advocate in the middle of the twentieth century, just as Whitman had in the middle of the nineteenth century. I'm definitely part of that tradition—definitely part of that great tree. I see myself as a branch on the tree of Whitman. There are many, many branches.

Now, 150 years later, what would you say are the key points to Whitman's legacy from *Leaves of Grass*, and who are its contemporary inheritors?
There are many things to take away from *Leaves of Grass* 150 years later, one of which is that Whitman is a poet of faith. His

faith, however, is not faith in God: it's faith in democracy, and faith in poetry, the power of poetry to change people and change the world. We need that kind of faith right now, at a time when democracy is being challenged by those who claim to uphold it, challenged by those who make war in the name of democracy.

We also need faith in poetry. Poetry has become so marginalized in this country, to the point of being mocked. It's not a coincidence that this is happening at a time when we need dissident voices, at a time when we need people to speak up. It's not a coincidence that poetry is so derided, because it's one vehicle by which those dissident voices might be heard.

Looking at *Leaves of Grass,* I am immediately struck by Whitman's faith both in poetry and in democracy. It's a faith that we need to reassert. I think the universal compassion expressed in *Leaves of Grass* must be reasserted. This is another timely lesson. It's not a coincidence that certain kinds of subjects recur throughout his work, especially in "Song of Myself." We can see the pattern: prisoners, prostitutes, and slaves keep cropping up in Whitman's verse. (He defends immigrants, too.) He makes repeated statements of solidarity with these most marginalized of people. We need more of that solidarity today. Whitman also had a deep appreciation for work, and for the working class in this country.

Finally, on an aesthetic level, one of the striking things about *Leaves of Grass* 150 years later is that we understand it with such immediacy. It's accessible. It's clear. It's direct. There is an aesthetic statement here that poetry should communicate, that it should clarify, instead of moving in the opposite direction. As you well know, too many poets today believe in obscurity for the sake of obscurity, weirdness for the sake of weirdness. That only serves to further alienate people from poetry, and rightly so. Poets complain about lacking an audience, and then write incomprehensible poems. They have no one to blame but themselves if that's what they choose to do.

Whitman did not do that. Whitman wanted to communicate. There is an urgency about Whitman's voice. There are good reasons why we're talking about this work now. There are good reasons why it's still relevant even though it was written 150 years ago, when so many poems written 150 days ago are no longer relevant.

Recently, an article surfaced where Whitman was quoted as saying, "don't be a poet" to the two young reporters who came to visit him. In the context of the article, where he also discussed the importance of learning the complete craft of writing, from typesetting to aspects of self-publishing and door-to-door distribution, it appeared as though Whitman was providing a blueprint for writers, particularly poets, to break with convention and forge into new territory of individual celebration as a writer or artist. Do you think Whitman consciously approached poetry from this point of view throughout his life?

It's striking that Whitman would insist upon learning all aspects of printing and publishing in addition to writing, per se. If you look at Whitman's work you see that it's very physical, very visceral. Whitman believed in evoking the senses. If you look at a poem like, "Crossing Brooklyn Ferry," you can still feel that. That's why Whitman can speak to the future reader. In essence, he says, "just as I do this today, you will do this" or "just as you do that today, so I did that." He's well aware of communicating with the future reader, and he can do that because his work is so steeped in the senses. He knows that we'll still be experiencing life in fundamentally the same way a century and a half later. It's not surprising to me that he would insist on knowing and understanding the physical part of making a poem or making a book.

I learned a long time ago how to make a book. My first book came out in 1982, when the process was very different, but I know the steps. Of course, I have to argue about everything. My father is the same way. He is a professional photographer, and he insists on understanding and teaching the entire process of making a print as part of a larger creative process. To him, they're inseparable. There is a very definite connection between snapping the photograph, developing the photograph into a print, then framing the photograph. It's all of a piece. I understand that approach.

Whitman's advice, "don't be a poet," sounds a bit tongue-in-cheek, and it's important to keep in mind that not everything he said can be taken at face value. Certainly, late in life, he said some things that would strike us as controversial or just plain wrong. Some of them he said in the company of his devoted friend, Horace Traubel. Traubel is an interesting character. He was a socialist who read Whitman's work from a socialist point of view, and argued for that reading with Whitman, who eventually conceded that his work was more socialist than he had previously admitted.

At the same time, Traubel was so devoted to Whitman that he recorded almost every utterance that came out of Whitman in the last few years of his life in Camden, New Jersey. Not all that is flattering, to say the least, and some of it was undoubtedly produced by the "good gray poet" as he was losing his grip on what we call reality. I still think it's important to read Whitman the way Traubel read him, but we also have to guard against interpreting every single utterance of Whitman as gospel.

I heard you read last year in Boston at a Boston Adult Literacy benefit, and you opened with a Spanish translation of number 24 from "Song of Myself." Do you ever see yourself undertaking a project in your writing similar to what Whitman did with *Leaves of Grass*? Will we ever see an Espada translation of *Leaves of Grass* in its entirety?

I enjoy reading Whitman aloud in Spanish. Whitman runs both north and south. He was introduced to Latin America and the Spanish-speaking world through José Martí and Rubén Darío. Later on, of course, Neruda became Whitman's greatest disciple in the Spanish language. Whitman influenced many poets in Latin America; at one point, he arguably had more influence in Latin America than he did in this country.

He is a poet who appeals to Latin America because he is wrestling with some of the great questions that still bedevil Latin America today, including national identity. His thirst for justice has considerable appeal in Latin America, particularly among writers and artists. It's not surprising to see that he had the effect he did in the Spanish language.

I would never presume to translate Whitman into Spanish myself. I am bilingual, but English is my first language and Spanish my second language. I was born in Brooklyn, and there are places in Brooklyn where English is still spoken.

In any case, I see very few poets undertaking the kind of epic project that is *Leaves of Grass*. Neruda certainly did it with *Canto General;* if anything, that work is even more vast than *Leaves of Grass*. Such an epic project is rare, and understandably so. I content myself with trying to understand things on a much smaller scale.

I see and hear Whitman's influence in many of your works, most notably the poem "Alabanza," and many of the poems from *Imagine the Angels of Bread*. What poems of yours do you see as distinctly Whitmanian?
Whenever I write about work, I hear Whitman's voice. The work could be my own or someone else's work. "I Hear America Singing" is in my head and will never leave. When I write about people who are incarcerated, I hear Whitman's voice. I've written a number of prison poems, based to a large extent on my own experience working as lawyer, or as a poet, with people who have been incarcerated.

I've written one poem where I speak directly of Whitman. It's a poem called, "Another Nameless Prostitute Says the Man Is Innocent." This is a poem for and about Mumia Abu-Jamal, the African-American journalist on death row in the state of Pennsylvania. Whitman makes an appearance because I visited his tomb in Camden, New Jersey, in 1997, and incorporated that visit into the poem I was writing about Mumia. This poem, by the way, was solicited by "All Things Considered" at National Public Radio and then censored by NPR. They refused to air it, which led to a public blow-up, I'm proud to say. Thus, Whitman made a very direct appearance—not by coincidence—in a poem about an African-American on death row. I think he would have appreciated that connection.

There are ways Whitman influences me that I have not yet discovered for myself. He is that pervasive. When he says, at the end of "Song of Myself," "look for me under your bootsoles," he's not simply trying to get our attention. He is saying that he is part of the world we inhabit and walk upon. I believe that. I come back to the fact that we are not ready for Whitman. Whitman gives good advice, which we have not yet followed. In the workshop today, I'm going to talk about another passage from his preface to the 1855 edition of *Leaves*, which has everything to do with how to live in the world. Beyond poetry, beyond politics, Whitman has advice for us on how to live every day. I think we should start listening to him.

There is a larger context for this conversation: so much is happening in this society that Whitman would absolutely condemn. Some of it is happening in poetry. Look at the movement toward obscurity, toward a trivialization of poetry, where the goal is to adopt a pose of detached, hip cynicism and not to engage with the world. Whitman is deeply engaged with the world; you get the sense that he's very involved. He's bombarded by the sensations of being alive, and he wants to share that with us immediately. He can't hold back. It has to emerge somehow.

We see, especially in the MFA universe, poets fleeing from the Whitman model, running in the opposite direction, towards what I don't know. It's a flight from anything that could move people, from anything that could change people. Whitman will be there no matter what they do. They could set fire to the whole forest and that's the one tree that won't burn down. It's that solid; it's that real.

You have to wonder: where's everyone going? Why are many poets, in MFA programs especially, fleeing from Whitman and what he represents? Why is it that there are too many MFA programs that barely teach Whitman, and do not teach his descendants? Why is it that so many MFA programs offer us only a model of obscurity? What's happening to American poetry that's so anti-Whitman? That's something to consider. Ultimately, when we see any cultural trend that can't be readily explained, we have to follow the money trail. We have to ask ourselves: Where are the dollars? The aesthetic of obscurity is rewarded in this country as it never has been before, in the form of all the resources we're familiar with: the grants, the awards, the residencies, the teaching appointments, and so on.

Again, Whitman is a poet of urgency, a poet of true communication, which is why we're still reading him today. His approach to the world is so spontaneous and tangible. You have to wonder why so many other poets went the other way.

I have to tell you: when I went to that reading in Boston, it marked a very pivotal shift in my own career, because I was seeing and hearing so much of this homogenized movement in contemporary poetry. I come from a tradition of Whitman, and that's what attracted me to writing: his style and what he had to say. When I heard you read, it really restored my faith. I know there is still a grounding and acknowledgment of traditional (Whitmanian) roots in this country. Prior to this, I was seeing so much fragmentation, a future of hopelessness in modern poetry.

The larger question here is: how do we make history? Who writes history? Who decides what history to include and what history to exclude? So often we accept the taken-for-granted reality. We accept the received wisdom without looking beyond those borders. We have to go beyond those borders to see Whitman, because Whitman is still an outlaw poet. Whitman is still a poet who represents certain values, which, if adopted, would radically transform this society. This goes beyond poetry. If we adopted the radical egalitarianism that Whitman expresses in "Song of Myself," let's say, or in *Leaves of Grass* more generally, this society would look very different. If we were to accept Whitman's sexuality, what would that do to the so-called "red states"? Half the preachers would be out of a job; half the politicians would be out of work. We're still arguing about whether or not the Confederate flag should be flown. What would Whitman make of that, the anti-slavery Whitman, the Whitman who wrote, "I Sing the Body Electric," that extraordinary anti-slavery poem? What would Whitman say about the people who still wave the Confederate flag a century and a half later? What would the Whitman of the Civil War, the Whitman of *Drum Taps,* the Whitman who was a nurse taking care of dying soldiers, make of those who romanticize the Confederate cause today, who still support the principles on which that Confederacy was founded? I think he would be aghast.

One of the most important interpretations I've read of Whitman is an essay written by the African-American poet June Jordan. Jordan wrote an essay called, "For the Sake of a People's Poetry: Walt Whitman and the Rest of Us." There, for the first time, I saw Jordan make explicit the connection between Whitman and poets of color. Of course, there is a precedent for this connection, because Langston Hughes echoed those same sentiments during his day. He was a poet of Whitman, and he declared himself to be in that camp. To him, there was no contradiction between being a poet of the Harlem Renaissance and a poet in the tradition of Whitman. In the same way, I see myself as a Latino poet, a Puerto Rican poet, a poet coming out of the so-called "Nuyorican" experience, and a poet in the tradition of Whitman. There is no contradiction. There, to this day, is where Whitman gets his greatest reception in the poetry world: on the margins, on the fringes, in the places where poets understand what it means to be silenced or suppressed or neglected. There Whitman lives and breathes.

We're going to celebrate Whitman this year because of the 150th anniversary of *Leaves,* but how many of us are going to read him? Of those who read him, how many will really take those words to heart? This is the poet who says he stands for "the rights of them the others are down upon." How many of us believe in those rights, and stand up for them?

I remember also, after having seen you on "NewsHour," that you appeared to have quite a collection of various editions of *Leaves of Grass.*
I discovered, after a while, that you can walk into a used bookstore and find a beat-up edition of Whitman from the 1930s or '40s for next to nothing, and that they make good companions. I started collecting them. It's remarkable to see how many different editions of Whitman have been produced.

One of the most remarkable is an edition called *American Bard.* This is the original preface, and the preface only, from the first edition of *Leaves of Grass.* It was edited and published by a poet and printer named William Everson (also known as Brother Antoninus), who felt that the preface from *Leaves* really is poetry, too. He took that prose, broke it down into verses, organized it with line breaks and stanza breaks, and shaped a poem from the preface. It's fascinating to see. It was an inspired way of calling attention to a piece of writing that had been overlooked because it wasn't included in the body of poetry, per se, and omitted in subsequent editions of *Leaves.* I have a few things like that in my library. Of course, I could never afford a signed edition of Whitman. That's out of my league.

It's great to see the way people respond to Whitman. Consider the assumptions we so often make about poetry based on Auden's famous phrase, "poetry makes nothing happen." That's become an article of faith among so many poets whose work, indeed, makes nothing happen. But I won't soon forget being in Chile last July (2004), at Isla Negra, Neruda's home on the Pacific coast, the day before his centenary. There was a huge gathering there, thousands of people, including a number of people who were there to visit his tomb. I went to his tomb. As part of the festivities, I was being videotaped. I decided to read the same passage you heard me read in Boston: number 24 from "Song of Myself"—in Spanish—at Neruda's tomb. Strangely, it felt like I was reading to a sick friend. A very sick friend. A dead friend, in fact. I read that passage out loud at the tomb of Neruda. I got through reading it and heard applause. I looked up; I was surrounded by people, listening. They were listening to Whitman in Spanish; it was remarkable to see their response that day at Neruda's tomb. It was as if they understood that the voice of Neruda's grandfather had just come calling. That's how Neruda felt about Whitman.

You are also heavily involved in the educational aspects of poetry. Do you find that many of your students are separated from connections to Whitman or the Whitmanic tradition?
A few of them have had Whitman shoved down their throats, and they didn't appreciate it. When Whitman is taught, especially at the high school level, I would imagine that there's some sanitizing going on. I am also quite sure that, over the years, as teachers took the path of least resistance, they would end up teaching some of Whitman's lesser work like, "O Captain! My Captain!"—the poem about Lincoln—and avoiding some of the more challenging work. How, over the years, in the Southern states for example, would you teach the passages from "Song of Myself" where Whitman identifies so closely with the fugitive slave? There's one point at which Whitman embraces a fugitive slave who comes to seek refuge at his house. It's a fictional event, but still a significant statement for Whitman to make in

the poem. There's another point at which Whitman actually transfuses himself into the body of a runaway slave—becomes a runaway slave—who is subsequently caught. How was that taught during all the years of segregation in the South? How is that taught today, anywhere, North or South?

I'm participating in a Whitman conference called "Look Back at Me" at Central Connecticut State University this coming September (2005). I know that every year there is a walk across the Brooklyn Bridge organized by the Poets' House where Galway Kinnell reads "Crossing Brooklyn Ferry." That is a remarkable poem, because he looks at the seagulls and knows that, crossing the same body of water, we will look up at the sky and see the same birds.

We should celebrate Whitman all the time, not just this year. A couple of years ago, I did a reading for the Smith College Poetry Center with Galway Kinnell and Kate Rushin to celebrate Whitman, and there was no particular occasion because we didn't need one.

I recently read Kinnell's *Book of Nightmares* and thought it was over the top; I loved it.
He's an important inheritor of the Whitman tradition, and someone who has written very intelligently about Whitman, too.

Who do you think are some of the other modern poets of this tradition?
I see a number of poets in that tradition. In North America, we go back to the beginning of the twentieth century and see Carl Sandburg, who is definitely part of the Whitman tradition. Edgar Lee Masters is definitely part of the Whitman tradition. Langston Hughes is definitely part of the Whitman tradition. Sterling Brown was influenced by Whitman. Of course, we all know about the Beats, about Ginsberg, [Gregory] Corso, and [Lawrence] Ferlinghetti, being devotees of Whitman.

I see it in Latino poets, especially in Chicano poets like Jimmy Santiago Baca, who came out of the prison experience. His early poems resonate with the Whitman influence. Feminist poets like Marge Piercy, poets who write about the body, who write very physically, come out of the Whitman tradition.

I think of Sharon Olds as very much a poet in the Whitman tradition, for the same reasons. I think of gay poets like Rafael Campo and Mark Doty as poets in the Whitman tradition. Obviously, the political poets—we think, immediately, of Carolyn Forché or Sam Hamill—are influenced by the Whitman inheritance.

That's why I go back to the image of the tree. It's not just that we have the strong roots and the strong foundation of Whitman; there are so many branches. All the poets that we're talking about constitute one branch or another of Whitman's tree.

Seers Unseen

The Poets of the Viet Nam War

There are neglected prophets among us, seers unseen. They have predicted one of the cataclysms of our time, and their message has been shunned by all but a few. These are the poets of the Viet Nam War, particularly the veterans who returned home to this country, turned against that war, and have been writing about this revelation ever since.

There is no more compelling way to confirm that history is repeating itself in Iraq and Afghanistan than to read the poets of the Viet Nam War: Doug Anderson, George Evans, Leroy Quintana, Yusef Komunyakaa, Bruce Weigl, Kevin Bowen, Lamont Steptoe, David Plumb, William Ehrhart, Michael Casey, and others. They speak with great moral force, a bitter wisdom rendered all the more tragic because it is so rarely acknowledged. The renunciation of war by veterans requires extraordinary courage; some have dealt with family ostracism, others with death threats. Indeed, no one knows or asks how many anti-war veterans have been spat upon over the years.

Viet Nam, of course, is still relevant more than three decades after that war ended. The struggle over the meaning of the war was a decisive factor in the 2004 presidential election, as demonstrated by the slanders of the Swift Boat veterans and the spectacle of Democratic candidate John Kerry fleeing from his finest hour as a veteran who protested the war. Now the wars in Iraq and Afghanistan lurch into another year. The poets warned us about what would happen in almost every particular.

For example, consider recruitment for this "volunteer" army. We have witnessed how, in the present day, the military is romanticized—and cunningly de-romanticized—to lure economically and emotionally vulnerable young people into its ranks. Here is Chicano poet and Viet Nam veteran Leroy Quintana, speaking of the same tactics nearly fifty years ago:

Armed Forces Recruitment Day,
Albuquerque High School, 1962

> After the Navy,
> the Air Force, and
> the Army,
> Sgt. Castillo,
> the Marine Corps
> recruiter,
> got a standing ovation
> when he walked up
> to the microphone
> and said proudly
> that unlike
> the rest, all
> he could promise
> was a pack,
> a rifle, and
> a damned hard time.
> Except for that,
> he was the
> biggest
> of liars.

Note Quintana's use of the word *liars.* This is strong stuff, but he has earned the right to use such language. If anything, Quintana reminds us that we are *too* concerned with the civility of public discourse, that there are times when we should call the liars by their true names. This is also an echo of "The old Lie" named by World War I poet Wilfred Owen: "Dulce et Decorum Est pro Patria Mori" (how sweet and decorous it is to die for one's country).

Consider, too, the prison scandal of Abu Ghraib, dramatized by the pathological photographs of inmates in hoods being humiliated and tortured at the hands of U.S. troops. Our government would have us believe that this is an anomaly, that these cruelties are not the natural outgrowth of greater cruelties inherent in military invasion and occupation. Witness, however, this account from the war in Viet Nam, by Yusef Komunyakaa:

Prisoners

Usually at the helipad
I see them stumble-dance
across the hot asphalt
with crokersacks over their heads,
moving toward the interrogation huts,
thin-framed as box kites
of sticks & black silk
anticipating a hard wind
that'll tug & snatch them
out into space . . .
Who can cry for them?
I've heard the old ones
are the hardest to break.
An arm twist, a combat boot
against the skull, a .45
jabbed into the mouth, nothing
works. When they start talking
with ancestors faint as camphor
smoke in pagodas, you know
you'll have to kill them
to get an answer . . .

The parallels are inescapable: the hoods, the thin bodies, the
boot against the skull. These images force us to acknowledge
that the concept of a benevolent occupation is oxymoronic, that
colonialism is colonialism, that it always comes to this.

As the civilian dead in Iraq and Afghanistan multiply—the famous Lancet study estimated 100,000 dead in Iraq, and even
cautious estimates number in the tens of thousands—we need
only read the poems written by North American veterans of the
Viet Nam war to see that we were warned about this, too. Doug
Anderson, a medic during the war, learned that "xin loi" means
"I'm sorry" in Vietnamese.

Xin Loi

The man and woman, Vietnamese,
come up the hill,
carry something slung between them on a bamboo mat,
unroll it at my feet:

the child, iron gray, long dead,
flies have made him home.
His wounds are from artillery shrapnel.
The man and woman look as if they are cast
from the same iron as their dead son,
so rooted are they in the mud.
There is nothing to say,
nothing in my medical bag, nothing in my mind.
A monsoon cloud hangs above,
its belly torn open on a mountain.

Rather than dealing in huge and unfathomable abstractions, Anderson gives the three million Vietnamese who died in that war a single human form, literally laid at his feet. In doing so, he has reversed the process of dehumanization that occurs as a prerequisite to slaughter. (The stubborn resourcefulness of racism should not be underestimated in this process. The "gooks" of 1965 have become the "ragheads" of 2010.)

Soldiers coming back from Iraq and Afghanistan are haunted now in the same way that soldiers have always been haunted, in same way that the veterans of Viet Nam are still haunted. George Evans writes:

Two Girls

That day I reached and swept the flies from the face of a
    Vietnamese
girl on the bed of a pickup truck, until I realized she was
    dead and
stopped, is the day I will never forget. Of all days, that is
    the day.

They crowded her eyes, until her eyes were as black and
    swirling and
indecipherable as the eyes of Edvard Munch's *Madonna*.

When I backed off, the whirlpool revealed such beauty my
    spine
melted. Such beauty I thought I couldn't live another
    moment. Such
beauty my soul dissolved. My heart died and revived, died
    and
revived, died and revived . . .

Elsewhere, Evans has written of Viet Nam that "Your ghosts are driving us out of our minds," pointing out that the Vietnam Veterans Memorial in Washington, D.C., would become "a black river that would surge across the country if it listed everyone ruined on every side."

Doug Anderson makes a similar observation in his poem, "The Wall": "How long a wall," he wonders, "if we inscribe three million Vietnamese, four million Cambodians, how long a wall?" Anderson fills "The Wall" with the kind of graphic detail that should give pause to any patriot eager to trumpet Owen's "old Lie:"

> I move my finger down the index, find the name of the first
> man
> I could not help, and for a moment, the tree splintering
> in front of me, smell of blood and cordite, his lips turning
> blue,
> the gasp of a lung filling with blood.

Yusef Komunyakaa calls his poem about the Wall "Facing It," a title that resonates on multiple levels, urging us to confront the consequences of war. Komunyakaa records his own presence at this place of grieving, like a painter rendering a self-portrait:

> My black face fades,
> hiding inside the black granite.
> I said I wouldn't, dammit:
> no tears.

By poem's end, Komunyaaka comes full circle, through images of blackness, to embrace the grieving of others, the private, yet public rituals of suffering he witnesses at the Wall:

> . . . In the black mirror
> a woman's trying to erase names:
> No, she's brushing a boy's hair.

For many of these veteran poets, the struggles continue, economically as well as emotionally. Viet Nam veteran poets, as a rule, do not hold tenured positions at major universities or publish with big New York houses. Some still scratch out a living, fighting off Post-Traumatic Stress Disorder or the debilitating effects of Agent Orange. With the notable exception of Komunyakaa, who won a Pulitzer Prize for *Neon Vernacular*, most veteran poets have been marginalized and ignored in the poetry world, and even, ironically enough, in the anti-war movement.

Left to their own devices, the veteran poets have organized themselves. The William Joiner Center for the Study of War and Social Consequences at the University of Massachusetts–Boston, directed by Kevin Bowen, hosts an annual writers' conference in June, featuring veteran writers and peace activists who teach workshops, deliver lectures, participate in panels, and give readings. The conference is not exclusive to veterans; I have served on the Joiner Center faculty every summer for more than a decade.

The writers of the Joiner Center are at the forefront of the initiative to normalize relations with Viet Nam. Kevin Bowen brings his counterparts—the *other* Viet Nam veteran poets, who were once his enemies—to the annual conference. Bowen has visited Viet Nam multiple times. To him, "Viet Nam" is not merely a war or an era, but a culture and a people, fully human:

River Music

One by one the lanterns
swim off down river.
A green one first, then red
and yellow. Each one calls
back a friend. Like dancers
they turn in circles.
One for my wife, one for my son,
one for our new child in spring.
Back and forth they swing
in twos and threes, seeking
ever newer combinations.
We drink rice liquor, toast
ten reasons men fall
in love on the river.
The old men smile into their instruments.
A woman sings, such beauty
even the moon might die
on her shoulder.

Some day future generations of veterans may write such poems for Iraq, but today "Iraq" is synonymous with war, the consequence of calculated amnesia. As Evans puts it: "We can't afford to heal. If we do, we'll forget, and if we forget, it will start again." Thus they continue to warn, as poets and prophets must. Owen, killed in France a week before Armistice Day at the age of twenty-five, expressed the same sense of urgency in the foreword to his posthumous collection of poems: "All a poet can do today is warn. That is why the true Poets must be truthful."

Ultimately, these are poets who do battle against the Cassandra Curse, gifted with prophecy but doomed, it seems, to go unheeded. This last poem of my own is a tribute to their persistence.

Blues for the Soldiers Who Told You

"I'm like a country who can't remember the last war."
  Doug Anderson

They told you that the enemy and the liberated throng
swaddle themselves in the same robes and rags,
wear the same masks with eyes that follow you,
pray in the same bewildering tongue, until your rifle
trembles to rake the faces at every checkpoint.
They told you about the corpse of a boy or girl
rolled at your feet, hair gray with the powder
of rubble and bombardment, flies a whirlpool blackening
    both eyes,
said you'll learn the words for apology too late to join
the ceremony, as flies become the chorus of your
    nightmares.
They told you about the double amputee from your town,
legs lopped off by the blast, his basketball friend
bumping home in a flag-draped coffin
the cameras will not film anymore,
about veterans who drench themselves in liquor
like monks pouring gasoline on their heads.

They told you in poems and stories
you did not read, or stopped reading
as your cheeks scorched with inexplicable fever,
and because they spoke with a clarity that burned your face,

because they saw with the vision of a telescope
revolving around the earth, they spent years wandering
through jails and bars, exiled to roads after midnight
where gas stations snap their lights off one by one,
seers unseen at the coffee shop waiting for bacon and eggs,
calling at 3 AM to say *I can't stop writing and you have to hear
   this.*
You will not hear this, even after the war is over
and the troops drown in a monsoon of desert flowers
tossed by the crowd, blooming in their mouths
to stop their tongues with the sweetness of it.

The Unacknowledged Legislator

A Rebuttal

Not long ago, I took part in a "beloved poems" panel at a poetry festival. I read Pablo Neruda in English and Spanish: Canto XII from *The Heights of Macchu Picchu*.

There were questions following the program. A member of the audience quoted Percy Bysshe Shelley and his famous dictum that, "Poets are the unacknowledged legislators of the World." The questioner asked the poets on the panel: Were we, in fact, the unacknowledged legislators of the world? Should poets literally become legislators?

What the poets in my workshop group recall was the tone of the response from the panel: "sneering . . . grumbling . . . less than gracious . . . snide and condescending." Several panelists mocked the whole idea of poets as "legislators," unacknowledged or otherwise, and, by extension, any form of political engagement for poets. It was a recitation from the scroll of received wisdom, well-known to British poet and editor Andy Croft: "poets need to get back in their box and stop meddling with things that don't concern them." One panelist in particular invoked the Poet Stereotype, raised on high like a crucifix in the face of a vampire: Poets were flaky, incompetent, irresponsible, narcissistic, naive, with political opinions that were uninformed at best and dangerous at worst. We couldn't be trusted to change a light bulb, much less change the world. This was all presented in the spirit of self-deprecation. *A legislator? Moi?* False modesty is to poets what ink is to octopi.

The Moderator for the panel heartily endorsed the collective sneer and chimed in with a sneer of his own. In the first-hand recollection of poet Rich Villar, the Moderator "specifically expressed gratitude that poets were not literally legislators since Neruda was a Stalinist, implying of course that Neruda would have been content to murder millions, the same way Stalin did." That casual, yet deliberate remark was intended to shut down the discourse, and it did. The Moderator moved on to the next question.

Yet the Moderator's grasp of the facts was, as academics are fond of saying these days, problematic. Pablo Neruda was not only a legislator; he was an extraordinary legislator. Poet Neruda was Senator Neruda in Chile from March, 1945 to January, 1948.

According to Adam Feinstein, in his biography *Pablo Neruda: A Passion for Life,* the poet ran for Senator on the Communist Party ticket in "the arid northern provinces of Tarapacá and Antofagasta in the Atacama desert, the driest region on Earth, where there was sometimes no rain for years on end." This was what Neruda called, "the great mining region of copper and nitrate," where his entire campaign consisted of a long poem to and about the miners, and these "men with scorched features" elected him in a landslide.

Neruda and the Communist Party in Chile—a labor party since its inception in 1922—supported the miners in various strikes, particularly a coal strike in the town of Lota. President Gabriel González Videla—elected with the backing of the Left in general and the Communists in particular—cracked down on the miners and the political party representing their interests.

Feinstein points out that "the Lota strike was perfectly legal, and it was nonsense to suggest that the Chilean communists were taking orders from Moscow." Nevertheless, in 1947 President González Videla outlawed the strike and the party, arresting hundreds, who were shipped to a concentration camp in Pisagua. Feinstein notes, with no small irony, that "among the men responsible for rounding up prisoners was a certain Augusto Pinochet Ugarte." Pinochet was appointed to run the Pisagua camp in early 1948, and took power in Chile years later following the military coup of September 11, 1973, becoming one of the most diabolical dictators in Latin American history.

In November 1947, Senator Neruda published an article in a Venezuelan newspaper condemning the repressive González

Videla regime and the appalling conditions endured by the miners. The day after the article appeared, President González Videla called for Neruda's ouster from the Senate. Instead, Neruda took to the Senate floor. As Feinstein tells it:

> On 6 January 1948, Pablo Neruda rose to his feet in the Senate and delivered one of the bravest, most astonishing speeches in Chilean political history. It has come to be known as "Yo acuso ("I Accuse")," after Zola's denunciation of the French government's persecution of the Jewish soldier, Alfred Dreyfus, fifty years earlier. "The President of the Republic has taken one more step in the unbridled political persecution which will make him notorious in the sad history of these days, by filing an action before the Supreme Court requesting my impeachment . . ."

Neruda then read aloud the names of all 628 people incarcerated at Pisagua without charge or trial. By the end of the month, he had disappeared, gone underground, a fugitive in his own country, passed from one safe house to another until he escaped across the Andes on horseback into Argentina more than a year later. He made his way to Paris, and turned up at the World Peace Congress in April, 1949, introduced by none other than Pablo Picasso. (The red-faced Chilean government announced that this alleged Neruda must be an imposter.) He was exiled until 1952.

This was Neruda the legislator, unacknowledged by the Moderator and our panel. We can only wonder how many elected officials in our House and Senate would dare to make such a speech from the floor of Congress; how many would say anything to risk re-election, much less imprisonment or execution; how many have ever demonstrated this kind of courage and integrity.

Neruda did put his faith in Stalin, like millions of communists around the world, until the Khrushchev revelations of Stalin's atrocities in February, 1956. At the time of his death in 1973, the *Collected Works* of Pablo Neruda numbered 3,522 pages. Like some vast mural, the poems teem with the faces of Latin American history, from the emperors to the stonehaulers, from the *conquistadores* to the revolutionaries. There is exactly one poem dedicated to Stalin, written on the occasion of the dictator's death. (It may be the worst poem ever written by a great poet.) There is a handful of other poems, such as "Let the Woodcutter Awaken," where Stalin is mentioned and praised. Yet, there are other, later poems where Neruda wrestles with his guilt and anguish over Stalin, like "Episodes," "Cult II," or "Elegy," a long work about Moscow, where he writes: "every garden had a hanged man." The poet sees "the geology of terror" in Stalin's face. There are no poems in praise of firing squads or slave labor camps, no poems that affirm what we would think of as Stalinist principles or tactics.

Roberto González Echevarría, in his introduction to the English-language edition of Neruda's *Canto General*, makes a useful comparison to Dante:

> We have long ago ceased to believe in Dante's vision (not a few crimes against humanity have been committed in the name of the Christianity he saw as the fulfillment of prophecy), and we still read his poem with reverence for the cohesion of his world-view as reflected in the poetic world he created. It is difficult, this close to the revelation of Stalin's abuses, to have the same distance from Neruda's vision.

At the height of the Cold War in the 1950s, Neruda was cranking out odes to French fries, salt, his socks, a hummingbird, a bricklayer, a laboratory technician, a bicycle, a village movie theater, a ship in a bottle, and a stamp album. By the end of the decade, he would publish one hundred love sonnets to his wife, Matilde. Shortly thereafter, he would translate *Romeo and Juliet* into Spanish.

To dismiss Neruda as a "Stalinist," then, and leave it at that, represents a grotesque distortion of poetry, politics, and history, worthy of the carnival mirror scene in *Lady From Shanghai*. In the words of Gregory Orr, poet and sympathetic fellow panelist, "Who can imagine reducing Neruda to any label, least of all compressing a lifetime of political engagement into a one word put-down?"

Robert Meeropol, the younger son of Julius and Ethel Rosenberg—who were executed by the U.S. government for allegedly conspiring to commit espionage by stealing the "secret" of the atomic bomb—has a truly unique perspective on communist politics in the 1940s and '50s. Meeropol says this about the politics of his parents—and, by inference, the politics of Neruda:

> My parents looked out their window and saw that the communists were the people doing good things in their neighborhood. They watched impoverished families with small children being kicked out of their apartments, having their possessions thrown in the street by landlords' goons because they couldn't pay the rent at the height of the Depression. They saw the Communist Party organize groups of people to move the families' possessions back in after the goons left . . . They went to Times Square for a big demonstration and saw mounted police charge through and beat peaceful demonstrators. They read the newspaper reports the next day that said the communists rioted and the police restored order. They knew the capitalist press lied. So they believed the Communist Party leaders when they said that the USSR was creating a workers' paradise, and they believed that the press lied when it described Stalin as a brutal dictator. Their error was extrapolating from their experience to things of which they had no direct knowledge. Given their experience, it was a reasonable extrapolation, and their actions were born out of a desire to make the world a better place for the vast majority of humanity.

Keep in mind the larger context for the politics of the Chilean poet: Communism was not the great political scourge of Latin America in the twentieth century; it was anti-communism. The ideology of anti-communism fueled the bloody military coup in Chile, the Dirty Wars in Argentina and Uruguay, the slaughter of thousands in El Salvador (in the 1930s and again in the 1970s), the forty-year Somoza dynasty in Nicaragua, the invasion of the Dominican Republic by U.S. Marines, and the continued colonial occupation of Puerto Rico. The ghost of anti-communism is always with us; sometimes he even shows up at gatherings of poets.

In *Revolutionary Memory: Recovering the Poetry of the American Left,* Cary Nelson notes that the emergence of political poetry as part of mainstream literary discourse was an accepted fact of life by the mid-1930s. The movement of the "proletarian poets" was in full swing, typified by Edwin Rolfe, the "Poet Laureate of the Abraham Lincoln Brigade," one of nearly three thousand American volunteers who fought in the Spanish Civil War against Franco and fascism; so, too, was the backlash, led by Allen Tate and his *Reactionary Essays on Poetry and Ideas*. According to Nelson, "Tate was fighting a rear guard action against cultural changes that seemed unstoppable . . . Eventually, Tate's position ceased to be one that had to be argued; it became an article of faith . . . The obvious inferiority of political poetry could be stated briefly on the assumption that other academic readers would agree." What happened?

McCarthyism happened. The Cold War happened. Poets were not exempt. Edwin Rolfe, working as a screenwriter, was blacklisted after the House Un-American Activities Committee begin investigating Hollywood in 1947; the movie of his novel *The Glass Room,* starring Humphrey Bogart and Lauren Bacall, never went into production. John Beecher was fired from San Francisco State College in 1950 for refusing to sign a loyalty oath; he was reinstated twenty-seven years later. Thomas McGrath was fired from Los Angeles State College in 1953 after his appearance as an "unfriendly witness" before HUAC; he ended up working for a company that manufactured carved wooden animals. Walter Lowenfels was charged with conspiracy to overthrow the U.S. government, a violation of the Smith Act; he was jailed in 1953 and convicted the following year, a conviction that was overturned on appeal.

Cary Nelson explains the ramifications for poets and poetry:

> It was a period of nationwide inquisition and fear. Thousands lost their jobs in extralegal hearings held by industry and by all levels of government. Some were imprisoned as well. The literature professorate protected itself by a theoretical severing of poetry and politics, and by a ruthless—sometimes condescending, sometimes frightened—purging of its and our historical memory. We have remained as a profession largely trapped within that ideology and that impoverished memory for more than thirty years. But we ceased to see it as ideology and instead lived it as one, as a self-evident fact of nature. Many of us forgot that there was a rich literary life beyond the stories we told about the discipline's favorite poems. And we

have forgotten that the restricted and depoliticized canon of modernism is effectively our discipline's testimony before HUAC. And we have continued, unwittingly, to repeat that testimony long after the committee has been discredited and disbanded. We are the products and the victims of a history we have forgotten.

This would explain the Moderator's knee-jerk Red-baiting at our panel, the implication that any poet who would dare to write political poetry or take political action was in danger of turning into a Commie pumpkin at midnight. This would explain, to a large degree, all that throat-clearing and eye-rolling in response to a perfectly intelligent inquiry. It was an energetic defense of apathy, but the man with the questions never did get his answers.

What did Shelley mean, anyway? Adrienne Rich, in her essay, "Poetry and Commitment," had this to say about Shelley and "unacknowledged legislators":

> I'll flash back to 1821: Shelley's claim, in "the Defence of Poetry" that "poets are the unacknowledged legislators of the world." Piously overquoted, mostly out of context, it's taken to suggest that simply by virtue of composing verse, poets exert some exemplary moral power—in a vague, unthreatening way. In fact, in his earlier political essay, "A Philosophic View of Reform," Shelley had written that "Poets *and philosophers* are the unacknowledged" etc. The philosophers he was talking about were revolutionary-minded: Thomas Paine, William Godwin, Voltaire, Mary Wollstonecraft.
>
> And Shelley was, no mistake, out to change the legislation of his time. For him there was no contradiction between poetry, political philosophy, and active confrontation with illegitimate authority . . .
>
> Shelley, in fact, saw powerful institutions, not original sin or "human nature," as the source of human misery. For him, art bore an integral relationship to the "struggle between Revolution and Oppression." His "West Wind" was the "trumpet of a prophecy," driving "dead thoughts . . . like withered leaves, to quicken a new birth."
>
> He did *not* say: "Poets are the unacknowledged interior decorators of the world."

By this definition, many of our greatest poets have been un-acknowledged legislators, from Shelley to Adrienne Rich her-self. This is what Whitman meant when he said: "I give the sign of democracy."

Poets should have no trouble identifying with being "unac-knowledged." They grouse about being ignored, about paltry attendance at readings and royalty statements that would cause most novelists to jump off a bridge. Yet poets also contribute to their marginalization by producing hermetic verse and living insular lives, confined to the academy or to circles of other poets, by mocking themselves as childish and unworldly, by refusing to embrace their role as unacknowledged legislators. The only antidote to irrelevancy is relevancy. The British poet Adrian Mitchell famously said: "Most people ignore most po-etry because most poetry ignores most people."

Mitchell lived his principles as a "mixed lefty," pacifist and un-acknowledged legislator; he was, in fact, declared the "Shadow Poet Laureate" of the United Kingdom. His poem, "To Whom It May Concern, " is an anti-war anthem. In February, 2003, he read to a quarter of a million people in the streets of London, gathered to protest the pending war in Iraq. In December, 2006, Mitchell was arrested and jailed for his part in a protest against the presence of the Trident nuclear submarine at a naval base in Faslane, Scotland. He was seventy-four years old at the time of his arrest; he died two years later.

His counterpart in the United States is poet, translator, and editor Sam Hamill. A former Marine and conscientious objec-tor, Hamill was invited to participate in a Bush White House symposium called, "Poetry and the American Voice," scheduled for February, 2003. That symposium was cancelled when word leaked out of Hamill's plan to collect a batch of anti-war poems and present them, like a bouquet of sorts, to First Lady Laura Bush. Hamill responded by organizing Poets Against the War. (The article has since been dropped; the organization is now called Poets Against War.)

Since its inception the organization has gathered more than 20,000 poems and statements against war; as Hamill puts it, "Never before in recorded history have so many poets spoken in a single chorus." The group is responsible for a website, a newsletter, and an anthology called *Poets Against the War* (Nation Books, 2003).

In the foreword to that anthology, Hamill writes:

> Can (thousands of) poems inhibit this or any administration planning a war? It is only one step among many. But it is an important step, as each is. We join physicians against the war, teachers against the war, farmers against the war, and others. Poets Against the War helped bring about hundreds of poetry readings and discussions around the world while compiling a document of historic proportion. And when our critics on the right suggest that poetry might somehow divorce itself from politics, we say, 'Read the Greeks, read the classical Chinese; tell it to Dante, Chaucer, Milton or Longfellow. Tell it to Whitman, Dickinson or Hughes. Tell it to García Lorca, to Joseph Brodsky or to the Chinese poets living in exile in our country . . . A government is a government of words, and when those words are used to mislead, to instill fear or to invite silence, it is the duty of every poet to speak fearlessly and clearly.

In "Dulce et Decorum Est," what provokes Wilfred Owen's wrath is not only the terrible reality of the trenches in World War I, but the cynical uses of language by government and other elites to incite the majority to act against its own interests. Our leaders no longer use Latin to celebrate patriotism and bombardment, but they still rely on a specialized vocabulary of war-mongering—and it works. The "weapons of mass destruction" were never found in Iraq, but the words themselves were destructive enough.

As Hamill puts it: "Since most poets write in the same language politicians are given to abuse, in the language of everyday common speech, they must struggle to reveal clarity by way of musical and imagistic expression, and by transparency of emotion." If phrases like *weapons of mass destruction* bleed language of its meaning, then poets must reconcile language with meaning and restore the blood to words. Owen uses the phrase *an ecstasy of fumbling* to describe the action of fitting on his gas mask before the deadly poison reaches him, then recalls a fellow soldier poisoned by the same gas with "white eyes writhing in his face." In such poems, as Gregory Orr observes, Owen takes back "the experience of war from the jabbering propagandists and patriots."

On January 27, 2007, my wife Katherine Gilbert-Espada, our son Klemente, and I marched in a demonstration with a delegation of unacknowledged legislators. DC Poets Against the War organized a poets' contingent as part of a United for Peace and Justice demonstration in Washington, D.C. Many in the poets' contingent wore placards created by my wife, with photographs of Langston Hughes, Wilfred Owen, Walt Whitman—and contemporaries like Doug Anderson and Daisy Zamora—accompanied by quotes from the poets. Marchers and onlookers stopped us on the street so they could "read" us, like books with legs.

I wore a Neruda placard bearing the last two stanzas from "I Explain a Few Things," one of his Spanish Civil War poems, written after the bombing of Madrid by fascist forces in 1936, when the aerial bombardment of civilians still had the capacity to shock the world. The translation is by Galway Kinnell:

> You will ask: why doesn't his poetry
> speak to us of dreams, of leaves,
> of the great volcanoes of his native land?
>
> Come and see the blood in the streets,
> come and see
> the blood in the streets,
> come and see the blood
> in the streets!

After the war ended in 1939, countless refugees fled from Spain, many facing imprisonment or execution. Thousands found themselves in French internment camps. Neruda helped buy a ship called the *Winnipeg,* and organized the evacuation of three thousand Spanish refugees from France to Chile. He called the *Winnipeg* "my greatest poem."

Chile celebrated the centenary of Neruda in July 2004. I was invited with a U.S. delegation to participate in the celebration. We visited Neruda's house at Isla Negra and his tomb overlooking the sea. That afternoon, about twenty people surrounded the tomb in a silent protest, carrying or wearing placards around their necks with the photos and names of the *desaparecidos,* the disappeared, killed and missing during the Pinochet dictatorship. Democracy had returned to Chile, but there was still no justice or peace of mind for the families of the disappeared, since the killers had never been punished and the bodies had never been found. They had become the conscience of the nation, proof that the democratic process was incomplete, pressuring the government to investigate these crimes and hold the guilty accountable. (Pinochet himself caused a furor by turning up at a used bookstore in Santiago a week before.)

To the families of the disappeared, it made perfect sense to seek justice at the tomb of a poet. Once they learned I was a poet, many of these grieving, dignified people spoke to me. This was the understanding of a poet's purpose that day at Isla Negra: They put their faith in the unacknowledged legislator.

Consider the state of our nation today, in a plummeting spiral after eight years of the Bush kleptocracy. Could poets do any worse than the legislators? Would poets strip away our constitutional rights in the name of security more vigorously than the lawyers who sit in the House and Senate? Would poets, those perfectionists of the word, so quickly and eagerly resort to corruptions of language like "enhanced interrogation" to describe torture, by way of explaining that some tortures (and torturers) are better than others? Would poets be any less ethical than the politicians who grovel before lobbyists for the insurance and drug companies, triggering a health care crisis without end? Would poets with empty pockets vote repeatedly to pour billions of dollars into one catastrophic war of plunder after another? Should poets leave politics to the Republicans and the Democrats, or should all of us—poets included—grapple with the world?

Shelley wrote in 1821 that poets are "the mirrors of the gigantic shadows which futurity casts upon the present." More than a century and a half later, in El Salvador, a poet and unacknowledged legislator by the name of Alfonso Quijada Urías would see the shadows and write (in this translation by Darwin Flakoll):

I content myself that some day
the owner of this poor grocery store
will make paper funnels
out of my writings
to wrap up his sugar and his coffee
for the people of the future
who now for obvious reasons
cannot savor his sugar or his coffee.

About Martín Espada

Called "*the* Latino poet of his generation" and "the Pablo Neruda of North American authors," Martín Espada was born in Brooklyn, New York, in 1957. He has published seventeen books in all as a poet, editor, essayist, and translator. A new collection of poems, *The Trouble Ball*, is forthcoming in 2011. *The Republic of Poetry*, a collection of poems published in 2006, received the Paterson Award for Sustained Literary Achievement and was a finalist for the Pulitzer Prize. Another collection, *Imagine the Angels of Bread* (1996), won an American Book Award and was a finalist for the National Book Critics Circle Award. Other books of poetry include *Crucifixion in the Plaza de Armas* (2008); *Alabanza: New and Selected Poems* (2003); *A Mayan Astronomer in Hell's Kitchen* (2000); *City of Coughing and Dead Radiators* (1993); and *Rebellion Is the Circle of a Lover's Hands* (1990). He has received numerous awards and fellowships, including the Robert Creeley Award, the Charity Randall Citation, the Paterson Poetry Prize, the Gustavus Myers Outstanding Book Award, the National Hispanic Cultural Center Literary Award, the Premio Fronterizo, two NEA Fellowships, the PEN/Revson Fellowship, and a Guggenheim Foundation Fellowship. His poems have appeared in the *The New Yorker, New York Times Book Review, Harper's, The Nation,* and *The Best American Poetry.* He has also published a collection of essays, *Zapata's Disciple* (1998); edited two anthologies, *Poetry Like Bread: Poets of the Political Imagination from Curbstone Press* (1994) and *El Coro: A Chorus of Latino and Latina Poetry* (1997); and released an audiobook of poetry called *Now the Dead will Dance the Mambo* (2004). His work has been translated into ten languages; collections of poems have recently been published in Spain,

Puerto Rico, and Chile. A former tenant lawyer, Espada is now a professor in the Department of English at the University of Massachusetts–Amherst, where he teaches creative writing and the work of Pablo Neruda.

Credits

Jack Agüeros, "Sonnet After Columbus, II," "Sonnet Substantially Like the Words of Fulano Rodríguez . . . ," "Psalm for Distribution," excerpts from "Sonnet for Heaven Below," "And He," and "Correspondence Between the Stonehaulers" from *Correspondence Between the Stonehaulers.* Copyright © 1991. "Sonnet for Ambiguous Captivity" from *Sonnets from the Puerto Rican.* Copyright © 1996. "Psalm for Amadou Diallo" from *Lord, Is This a Psalm?* Copyright © 2002. All reprinted with the permission of Hanging Loose Press.

Claribel Alegría, excerpt from "The Rivers" from *Luisa in Realityland,* translated by Darwin Flakoll. Copyright © 1987. Reprinted with the permission of Curbstone Press c/o Northwestern University Press.

Doug Anderson, "Xin Loi" and excerpt from "The Wall" from *The Moon Reflected Fire* (Alice James Books, 1994). Copyright © 1994 by Doug Anderson. Reprinted with the permission of the author.

Kevin Bowen, "River Music" from *Playing Basketball With the Viet Cong* (Curbstone Press, 1994). Originally published in *The Boston Review* 18, no. 2. Copyright © 1994 by Kevin Bowen. Reprinted with the permission of the author.

Sterling Brown, excerpt from "Remembering Nat Turner" from *The Collected Poems of Sterling A. Brown.* Copyright © 1980 by Sterling Brown. Reprinted with permission of Northwestern University Press.

Julia De Burgos, excerpts from "To Julia De Burgos," "23rd of September," and "Ours is the Hour" from *Song of the Simple Truth: The Complete Poems,* translated by Jack Agüeros. Copyright © 1997. Reprinted with the permission of Curbstone Press c/o Northwestern University Press.

Edward J. Carvalho, excerpts from "A Branch on the Tree of Whitman: Martín Espada on the 150th Anniversary of *Leaves of Grass*" (interview)

UNDER DISCUSSION
Annie Finch and Marilyn Hacker, General Editors
Donald Hall, Founding Editor

Volumes in the Under Discussion series collect reviews and essays about individual poets. The series is concerned with contemporary American and English poets about whom the consensus has not yet been formed and the final vote has not been taken. Titles in the series include: